THE EXCEPTIONAL TEACHER'S HANDBOOK

Second Edition

Second Edition

The Exceptional Teacher's Handbook

The First-Year Special Education
Teacher's Guide to Success

Carla F. Shelton • Alice B. Pollingue

CORWIN PRESS
A Sage Publications Company
Thousand Oaks, California

For information:

Corwin Press
A Sage Publications Company
2455 Teller Road
Thousand Oaks, California 91320
www.corwinpress.com

Sage Publications Ltd.
1 Oliver's Yard
55 City Road
London EC1Y 1SP
United Kingdom

Sage Publications India Pvt. Ltd.
B-42, Panchsheel Enclave
Post Box 4109
New Delhi 110 017 India

Printed in the United States of America

Library of Congress Cataloging-in-Publication Data

Shelton, Carla F.
The exceptional teacher's handbook: The first-year special education
teacher's guide to success / Carla F. Shelton and Alice B. Pollingue.— 2nd ed.
   p. cm.
Includes bibliographical references and index.
ISBN 0-7619-3195-3 (cloth) — ISBN 0-7619-3196-1 (pbk.)
  1. Special education—United States—Handbooks, manuals, etc. 2. Special
education teachers—United States—Handbooks, manuals, etc. 3. First year
teachers—United States—Handbooks, manuals, etc. I. Pollingue, Alice B. II. Title.
LC3969.S36 2005
371.9′0973—dc22

                                             2004018088

This book is printed on acid-free paper.

04   05   06   07   08   10 9 8 7 6 5 4 3 2 1

Acquisitions Editor:	Robert D. Clouse
Editorial Assistant:	Jingle Vea
Production Editor:	Julia Parnell/Diane S. Foster
Typesetter:	C&M Digitals (P) Ltd.
Proofreader:	Scott Oney
Indexer:	Judy Hunt
Graphic Designer:	Rose Storey

Contents

Preface

*T*he *Exceptional Teacher's Handbook* is a comprehensive resource book designed to assist and support the special education teacher through his or her first school year and new teaching experience. The handbook supplies the first-year teacher with a step-by-step management approach designed to improve and enhance his or her skills in the areas of organization, time management, and instructional planning and implementation. The resource book contains information on critical topics such as student placement, discipline, classroom management, transition, classroom organization and design, parent conferences, and professional development. In addition, the authors have included resources that supply the new teacher with a wealth of miscellaneous information ranging from first aid procedures in the school setting to techniques for stress management.

The handbook's contents are sequentially arranged in order to guide the new teacher from the initial planning stage prior to the start of school through the postplanning stage of the school year. The authors provide numerous time-saving checklists and miscellaneous forms that can be reproduced and will assist the beginning teacher in accomplishing the multitude of required tasks that are always present. The handbook is designed to be used as a quick reference; therefore, every chapter is written in an abbreviated format and can be reviewed in a matter of minutes. The chapters are structured in a manner that will provide the reader with current information on the chapter's topic, which is validated by research for most topics, followed by a "how-to-do-it" plan of action for the teacher when appropriate.

Finally, *The Exceptional Teacher's Handbook* can assist the first-year teacher in successfully navigating the ever-changing maze of the special education profession. The handbook was written from a classroom teacher's perspective and supplies the reader with practical suggestions. The contents of the book can be tailored to fit the individual needs of most special education programs or models and provide the beginning teacher with the necessary framework for a successful school year. The handbook is an indispensable resource that will guide and assist the new teacher throughout the entire school year. More important, the text will empower the first-year special education teacher with the confidence necessary to meet the challenge of the profession.

Corwin Press gratefully acknowledges the contributions of the following people:

Margaret H. Blackwell
Executive Director, Exceptional
    Education and Student Services
Chapel Hill–Carrboro City Schools
Chapel Hill, NC

Mary Ann Beckman
SPED Teacher
Greenfield High School
Greenfield, WI

Carole Campbell
Assistant Professor
Teacher Education With Specialties
    in Early Childhood Education
    and Early Childhood Special
    Education
Arkansas State University
State University, AR

Richard Cash
District Coordinator
    of Gifted and Talented
    Programs
Bloomington Public Schools
Bloomington, MN

Wanda Routier
SPED Teacher
Sugar Bush
    Elementary School
Greenville, WI

Carolyn Guess
Assistant Superintendent
    for Special Education
Houston, Texas Independent School
    District
Houston, TX

About the Authors

 **Carla F. Shelton**, Ed.S., has 11 years of teaching experience in the special education profession. She has taught students with disabilities in Grades 2 through 12 in resource, self-contained, and inclusion settings. She is certified in the areas of specific learning disabilities, emotional/behavior disorders, mildly intellectual disabilities, elementary grades (P–8), school counseling (P–12), and educational leadership and supervision. She has served as a high school counselor for the past 5 years working with students in Grades 9 through 12. She is the author of *Best Practices for Secondary School Counselors*. She is knowledgeable in instructional techniques and best classroom practices that promote and foster student learning. She is skilled in designing and implementing strategies designed to assist students with disabilities in meeting academic and behavior goals and objectives, to bridge the gap between school and parents, and to assist students with the transition process from school to school and to postsecondary endeavors. She has mastered the art of collaboration with general education teachers and staff and works effectively with families of students with disabilities. She has presented at the High Schools That Work Summer Conference, the National Tech Prep Conference, the Georgia School Counselor Conference, and the Association for Supervision and Curriculum Development Annual Conference. Her professional affiliations include the American School Counselor Association, Georgia School Counselor Association, National Tech Prep Network, and Professional Association of Georgia Educators. Her solid education background and broad-based educational experience are the foundation on which *The Exceptional Teacher's Handbook* is built.

Alice B. Pollingue, Ed.D., is Assistant Professor of Education at Augusta State University. She has been teaching at the university for more than 14 years. She teaches special education courses to undergraduate and graduate students and is the supervising professor for the entire special education teacher training program. She develops curriculum for new special education courses offered at the university. In addition, she is a consultant for school systems in the surrounding area. She has published articles in the *Journal of Early Education* and the *Journal of Special Education.* She is active in both local and national professional organizations. Her motivation, professionalism, knowledge, and expertise make her the perfect coauthor for *The Exceptional Teacher's Handbook.*

As a writing team, the authors bring solid professional credentials and expertise in the field of special education to this project. Their shared beliefs, philosophies, and love for the profession led to the writing of a book that epitomizes their common vision.

*Carla dedicates the second edition to
her mother, Faye West, for her love, support, and encouragement.
The authors thank the reviewers for their time and efforts on the revision of*
The Exceptional Teacher's Handbook. *Their feedback was the authors' compass throughout the endeavor.*

Introduction

The new special education teacher will find his or her first school year to be a time of transformation from novice to professional, and the experiences encountered during this period will be remembered for a lifetime. The metamorphosis from student to teacher finally occurs, and the time comes for the beginning teacher to apply all newly acquired knowledge and skills to his or her first teaching position. The journey through the first year is often filled with a tremendous amount of promise and excitement, but it also frequently contains unforeseen challenges that will threaten to dampen the new special education teacher's dedication and enthusiasm for the profession and possibly overshadow the most positive aspects of the first-year experience. All beginning teachers will experience some sort of difficulty during the first year. Gordon (1991, p. 5) found the following to be the most common needs of first-year general education teachers:

- Managing the classroom
- Acquiring information about the school system
- Obtaining instructional materials and resources
- Planning, organizing, and managing instruction and other professional responsibilities
- Assessing students and evaluating student progress
- Motivating students
- Using effective teaching methods
- Dealing with individual students' needs, interests, abilities, and problems
- Communicating with colleagues, including administrators, supervisors, and other teachers
- Communicating with parents
- Adjusting to the teaching environment and role
- Receiving emotional support

Current studies reveal that first-year special education teachers share some of the same concerns as first-year general education teachers. Whitaker (2001) states,

> Beginning special education teachers needed assistance in the following areas (from greatest reported need to least reported need): system information related to special education, emotional support, system information related to the school, materials, curriculum, and instruction, discipline, interactions with others, and management. (p. 5)

The recent changes in the Individuals with Disabilities Education Act and the passing of the No Child Left Behind Act are additional issues that new teachers are finding extremely intimidating and the source of tremendous stress. These issues are factors that may profoundly impact the decisions of first-year special education teachers to continue in the profession. School systems throughout the country must send a strong message to their school administrators to encourage and support these new professionals throughout their first year and continuously provide positive reinforcement when they exhibit the characteristics associated with excellence in the profession. A study of excellent first-year teachers found these individuals to possess the following defining characteristics:

1. Genuine concern regarding the welfare of their students

2. Commitment to the success of all children

3. Enduring enthusiasm

4. Consistently encouraging attitude

5. The resolve to not be intimidated by challenges (Daugherty, 2003, p. 2)

The second edition of *The Exceptional Teacher's Handbook* has been revised to address the issues previously mentioned and the most common needs of beginning special education teachers as identified by current research. The authors have added additional innovative strategies and current information pertaining to special education, and they have identified best practices that will promote the building of characteristics identified in excellent first-year teachers. The revisions are based on new developments in education and feedback from professionals in the field of special education who have reviewed the first edition. The major changes to the second edition are as follows:

• The authors have added thought-provoking quotes at the beginning of each chapter as a means to not only engage and motivate the reader but also encourage reflection on the chapter's contents.

• The authors provide the reader with researched-based information pertaining to a chapter's topic where appropriate that provides the reader with a solid frame of reference and supports the authors' strategies and/or suggestions pertaining to the topic.

• The authors have reorganized the contents of each chapter in an effort to improve the flow of the text and enable the reader to quickly locate needed information or supporting material.

The purpose of *The Exceptional Teacher's Handbook* is to provide the first-year special education teacher with the tools necessary to successfully make the transformation from novice to professional. The authors recognize that a tremendous amount of diversity exists among special education programs and delivery models; the basic concepts presented throughout the book, however, can be applied to most situations. The authors contend that successful teachers, regardless of area of certification, must possess the following to develop a culture of learning and promote academic achievement for all students:

- Excellent time management and organizational skills
- An in-depth understanding of students' needs
- The ability to manage the classroom and create a climate that promotes student learning
- The knowledge of teaching practices that result in an increase in students' academic performances and acquisition of essential skills
- The ability to prepare students for transition to the next level of education or experiences
- The initiative to design and implement a personal professional development plan that assists the teacher in staying current in his or her field

The contents of the book will assist the new teacher in his or her efforts to address each of these areas. The authors encourage the reader to use the book as a resource and guide as he or she begins to chart a course toward a successful first year.

Preparing for a Successful School Year

To begin with the end in mind means to start with a clear understanding of your destination. It means to know where you're going so that you better understand where you are now so that the steps you take are always in the right direction.

—Steven Covey

Preparation is the key to achieving a successful school year for the new special education teacher. The work habits and time management skills that beginning teachers employ during the first days of school set the tone for the remainder of the year. Traditionally, school systems begin the new school year with a preplanning time period designed to provide the opportunity for teachers to prepare for instruction, collaborate with colleagues, participate in staff development classes, and chart a general direction for the upcoming year. Frequently, the new special education teacher must use this time period to confirm his or her new class rosters, resolve transportation issues, select general education teachers for students in inclusion or mainstream environments, collaborate and plan with general education teachers, create or fine-tune students' schedules, select appropriate instructional materials, and create a class schedule that is conducive to the school's master schedule. The first-year special education teacher can often be found asking the question, "Where do I begin?"

In the following sections, the authors identify five strategies that they have found to be the building blocks for a successful school year. The authors discuss each strategy and provide the reader with the necessary supporting forms and checklists for successful implementation. The chapter includes basic information that will guide the teacher in his or her efforts to address matters ranging from resolving logistical issues to locating a mentor teacher. In addition, the authors suggest that the new teacher maintain a journal and make time for reflection throughout the school year. The beginning teacher will discover that each school year is unique, and preparation is the critical element for a successful and productive year.

STRATEGY 1: IDENTIFY ESSENTIAL TASKS

Beginning special education teachers should identify and prioritize all essential tasks that must be accomplished during the pre- and postplanning time periods and on a monthly basis throughout the school year. The authors have developed checklists of items for each period that will help the new teacher establish good work habits and time management skills and successfully complete his or her first year. The authors are aware that a tremendous amount of diversity exists among special education programs and delivery models; in light of this fact, however, there continue to be certain tasks that must be accomplished by the teacher of students with exceptionalities if the goal of a successful school year is to be achieved. The contents of every teacher checklist are broken down into four major categories:

- Special education administrative tasks
- General classroom/instructional tasks
- Noninstructional tasks
- Professional development

The authors recommend that the teacher review each checklist and select the tasks that are relevant and add additional tasks as needed to meet the individual needs of his or her students or program. The authors have created several forms to support the tasks outlined in the planning checklists.

Materials or Resources

Form 1.1: Preplanning Checklist

Form 1.2: Monthly Planning Checklist

Form 1.3: Postplanning Checklist

Form 1.4: Correspondence Log

Form 1.5: Student Emergency Information

Form 1.6: Noninstructional Classroom Supply Checklist

Form 1.7: Instructional Classroom Supply Checklist

Form 1.8: Classroom Inventory Checklist

Form 1.9: Student Information

Form 1.10: Present Levels of Performance

STRATEGY 2: ORIENT ASSIGNED PARAPROFESSIONALS

"Paraprofessionals are noncertified staff members who are employed to assist certified staff in carrying out the education programs and otherwise helping in the instruction of students with disabilities" (Friend & Bursuck, 2002, p. 103). The new teacher typically has the primary responsibility of orienting the paraprofessional assigned to his or her special education program. The teacher should include the following in his or her orientation session: Define the individual's role and responsibilities, outline classroom expectations and procedures, discuss the rules of confidentiality, take the paraprofessional on a tour of the school, review the school's faculty handbook, discuss basic school information, and preview the areas in which the paraprofessional will be evaluated at the end of the year. The teacher must emphasize that the paraprofessional is an important member of the special education team and plays an important role in facilitating the education process for students. Paraprofessionals need periodic feedback from the supervising teacher to address areas of concern and provide positive reinforcement for effective practices. Salend (2001) states,

> Feedback can include job performance, rapport with students and other school personnel, and information on how to work more effectively. You can also ask paraeducators and volunteers for their point of view about their roles in the school, and you can acknowledge their contributions with notes from students and teachers, graphs or other records of student progress, certificates of appreciation, and verbal comments. (p. 123)

The authors have developed a checklist of the most common responsibilities of paraprofessionals and have included a list of suggestions for working with these individuals. This information is located in the supplement forms and resource section of this chapter.

Materials or Resources

Form 1.11: Paraprofessional's Classroom Responsibilities Checklist

Resource 1.1: Suggestions for Working With a Paraprofessional

STRATEGY 3: ESTABLISH AND MAINTAIN COMMUNICATION WITH PARENTS AND STUDENTS

The special education teacher must establish and maintain communication with parents and students to establish rapport and build solid partnerships. The authors recommend the following activities to assist the new teacher in his or her efforts to implement an effective communication system:

- Conduct an Orientation Session

Orientation sessions provide the new teacher with an opportunity to establish communication with parents and students and can assist with setting the tone for the remainder of the school year. The best time to conduct an orientation session is prior to the start of the new school year. Teachers can take this opportunity to introduce all staff members who will be working with students, provide parents with a description of the special education program or model, discuss classroom expectations and procedures, preview academic curriculum and materials, and tour the school. The authors recommend that the teacher design a simple needs assessment survey to collect information from parents regarding areas of concern and educational topics of interest that can be addressed through future parent workshops. The teacher should provide an opportunity for parents to evaluate the orientation session to gain insight on the quality of the session and obtain information on areas that need improvement. The evaluation may consist of a pencil-and-paper instrument or a computer-assisted survey.

- Conduct Parent Workshops and Information Sessions

Parent workshops and information sessions assist the beginning teacher in building a bridge of understanding and communication with parents. Workshops allow parents to learn new skills and practice others, whereas information sessions provide parents with insight on specific topics of interest or concern. The authors recommend the following steps to plan a quality parent workshop:

Step 1: Select topic or focus.

Step 2: Select date, time, and location.

Step 3: Develop goals and objectives.

Step 4: Collect materials or coordinate to have a guest speaker.

Step 5: Develop an agenda.

Step 6: Advertise, advertise, and advertise.

Step 7: Develop an evaluation instrument.

- Create an Informative and User-Friendly Web Page

The creation of an informative, user-friendly Web page and e-mail account will maximize the new teacher's ability to disseminate and receive information from parents and students. "Technology can assist in communicating a message which can be received at the convenience of the target audience without the barriers of space, place, or time" (Sabella & Booker, 2003, p. 207). The authors found in their review of school Web sites in the United States that Web pages of teachers differ significantly in design, size, and type of information provided on a page. In light of this discovery, the authors developed three categories of information that they recommend for a teacher's Web page. The reader is cautioned that Web pages are best when kept simple in design and updated on a continuous basis. In addition, the teacher must remember that not every student and parent has access to technology, and critical information should continue to be distributed in a hard-copy format. The authors have included a multitude of Internet links that teachers can use when constructing their pages.

Recommended Web Page Information

1. Introduction of the special education teacher and staff
   a. Teacher and staff pictures (use digital camera)
   b. Teacher and staff biographies

    c. Teacher and staff telephone numbers with extensions

    d. Teacher and staff e-mail addresses

2. Classroom information

    a. Class schedule

    b. Classroom policies and procedures

    c. Syllabi for academic subjects (possibly by grading period)

    d. Weekly homework assignments

    e. Highlights of special projects

    f. Procedures for requesting a conference with the teacher

3. Parent and student information and resources

    a. Specific grade-level information

    b. Monthly class bulletin or newsletter (noting important dates and upcoming events, specific class information, specific academic or social skill of the month, and other tidbits)

    c. Web site links

        1. Parent support organizations

        2. Student support organizations

        3. Homework help for students

        4. College

        5. Financial aid and scholarships

        6. Career

        7. Career information for specific fields

        8. College entrance exams

Materials or Resources

Resource 1.12: Web Sites for Parents and Students

STRATEGY 4: LOCATE A MENTOR TEACHER

A mentor teacher can provide the beginning teacher with the emotional support that is helpful as he or she navigates through unfamiliar territory during the first year. A mentor is an individual who can provide the new teacher with valuable information pertaining to successful instructional strategies, serve as a role model, share knowledge and skills, provide support and encouragement, and, most important, listen. Daugherty (2003) reported in his survey of teachers who had been awarded the Sallie Mae Award, which is given by the American Association of School Administrators and the Student Loan Marketing Association to first-year teachers who have demonstrated superior instructional skills and exhibited excellent interaction with students, faculty, and parents, that "a majority of award winners emphasized the value of mentorship programs aimed at easing the transition from student or intern teacher to professional" (p. 460). Mentor programs have been found to enhance the retention of new special education teachers and appear to be the most effective when mentors have weekly contact with their new teachers (Fore, Martin, & Bender, 2002). The authors suggest that the new teacher find a mentor who is currently teaching in the same field and building to maximize the effectiveness of the mentoring program.

STRATEGY 5: ALLOCATE TIME FOR REFLECTING

The first-year special education teacher should allocate a sufficient amount of time for personal reflection throughout the school year. The authors recommend that the teacher maintain a journal and record daily or weekly thoughts and feelings pertaining to his or her experiences. The teacher will find this exercise to be one that not only relieves stress but also can provide insight into classroom practices that prove to be productive and identify those that definitely need to be "tweaked." In addition to maintaining a journal, the authors recommend that the beginning teacher conduct a self-evaluation at the end of the school year as a means to evaluate his or her first efforts as a professional educator. The authors provide the reader with a basic instrument that can be used by most special education teachers.

Materials or Resources

Form 1.12: Self-Evaluation Instrument for the Special Education Teacher

Form 1.1   Preplanning Checklist

I. Special Education Administrative Tasks

_____ Procure current class roster from special education director or special education county or district office.

_____ Procure current Individualized Education Programs (IEPs) from special education director or special education county/district office.

_____ Review all student IEPs and complete **Student Information** form (Form 1.9).

_____ Procure special education contact person's name and telephone number (possibly referred to as the special education coordinator).

_____ Contact school counselor and review students' schedules for the new school year.

_____ Coordinate with the school counselor and place students in general education classes as dictated by the IEP.

_____ Conference with teachers of students placed in inclusive settings.

_____ Complete **Classroom Adaptations** form and distribute to teachers of students placed in inclusion or mainstreamed settings (see Chapter 3).

_____ Distribute necessary student discipline information or addendums to the appropriate school administrator.

_____ Create **Correspondence Log** book to document all communications with parents, teachers, school administration, and other important sources (Form 1.4).

_____ Complete the **Paraprofessional's Classroom Responsibilities Checklist** and discuss with the paraprofessional assigned to your class. Be prepared to clarify and explain all assigned duties (Form 1.5).

II. Classroom/Instructional Tasks

_____ Procure school systems curriculum guide for subjects to be taught in the special education classroom and review material thoroughly.

_____ Review each student's IEP on the **Present Levels of Performance** form (Form 1.10).

_____ Establish a classroom schedule for academic instruction and exploratory/specialty activities.

_____ Procure instructional and supporting materials.

_____ Procure lesson plan and grade book.

_____ Plan lessons and organize instructional materials.

_____ Construct bulletin boards that reflect instructional units/themes.

(Continued)

Form 1.1 (Continued)

_____ Place emergency response and exit procedures in highly visible areas:

1. Fire drill
2. Tornado or inclement
3. Bomb threat
4. Other weather drill

_____ Establish classroom procedures and post in classroom:

1. Class rules and consequences
2. School grading scale
3. Class grading procedures and scale
4. Daily routine/schedule

_____ Prepare parent classroom information packet to be sent home the first day of class (see Chapter 4).

_____ Copy **Student Emergency Information** form to be completed the first day of class (Form 1.5).

III. Noninstructional Tasks

_____ Procure or request noninstructional supplies. Use the **Noninstructional Classroom Supply Checklist** (Form 1.6).

_____ Inventory the contents of the classroom. Use the **Classroom Inventory Checklist**, and record all serial numbers of major equipment and note the condition of all items listed below (Form 1.8):

1. Number of student desks
2. Teacher desk
3. Tables
4. Chairs
5. Book shelves
6. File cabinets
7. Storage cabinets
8. Computer
9. Computer table
10. Overhead projector
11. Carts
12. Tape recorders
13. Earphones/headsets
14. Televisions
15. VCRs
16. Printer

_____ Procure faculty duty roster and note all assigned duties and their dates, times, and locations.

IV. Professional Development

_____ Join at least one professional organization (see Chapter 10).

_____ Subscribe to at least one professional periodical (see Chapter 10).

_____ Procure a schedule of conferences related to special education and make arrangements to attend at least one conference per school year.

_____ Procure a schedule of staff development for certified personnel offered through the school system.

_____ Start current special education articles notebook (make copies of all articles of special interest and place in a three-ring binder).

_____ Obtain liability insurance for educators through a professional organization.

V. Additional Teacher Tasks

_____

_____

_____

_____

_____

_____

_____

_____

_____

_____

_____

_____

_____

_____

_____

_____

_____

_____

_____

_____

_____

Form 1.2   Monthly Planning Checklist

I. Special Education Administrative Tasks

_____ Review students' current Individualized Education Programs (IEPs).

_____ Annotate all mastered short-term objectives on students' current IEPs.

_____ Schedule annual review meetings for students whose IEP will expire within 30 days.

_____ Send **Student Monitor Information** forms to teachers of students placed in inclusive settings (see Chapter 3).

_____ Review all monitor results and record information on the **Student Monitor Results Summary** form (see Chapter 3).

_____ Review students' behavior plans/contracts and revise where necessary. The authors provide a generic **Behavior Contract** (see Chapter 4).

_____ Correspond with parents in reference to student progress in the general education classroom.

II. Classroom/Instructional Tasks

_____ Complete instructional plans.

_____ Procure materials to support instructional plans.

_____ Construct bulletin boards to reflect current instructional units or themes.

_____ Prepare progress reports or report cards.

_____ Communicate with parents in reference to student progress in the special education classroom.

III. Noninstructional Tasks

_____ Check noninstructional supplies and replenish as necessary.

_____ Review dates for designated faculty meetings or special education meetings.

IV. Professional Development Tasks

_____ Review professional journals, and copy articles of interest and place in a notebook for future reference.

_____ Select and read a book on an educational topic of interest.

_____ Attend professional conferences and staff development courses.

V. Additional Teacher Tasks

_____

_____

_____

_____

_____

Form 1.3 Postplanning Checklist

I. Special Education Administrative Tasks

_____ Review all students' Individualized Education Programs (IEPs) and ensure each plan is current and complete.

_____ Annotate all mastered goals and objectives on each student's IEP.

_____ All IEPs should be in a file folder and placed in a secured location (preferably a locking file cabinet).

_____ Send IEP folders of students being promoted to the next grade and changing schools to the new special education teacher (Example: Moving from elementary to middle school or moving from middle school to high school).

_____ Review each student's progress in all inclusive settings and record final grade.

_____ Inform parents of students' progress in general education classes.

_____ Contact school counselor and review students' schedules for the new school year. (This is especially important for high school students.)

_____ Coordinate with the school counselor and place students in general education classes for the new school year as dictated by their IEPs.

_____ Contact special education coordinator or special education director to obtain final instructions before leaving school for the summer.

II. Classroom/Instructional Tasks

_____ Prepare and complete final grades for all special education classes.

_____ Record final grades on students' permanent record or input final grades into school's student information system.

_____ Organize and store instructional materials.

_____ Remove and store all bulletin board materials and posters.

_____ Return all materials procured from the school media center or other faculty members.

_____ Follow school policy for closing out the school year. (Most schools will have a written checklist for teachers to follow before leaving for the summer.)

III. Noninstructional Tasks

_____ Complete noninstructional supplies form for new school year. Place order before leaving for the summer.

_____ Inventory classroom contents and note all deficiencies.

_____ Complete work order for broken equipment or classroom deficiencies.

(Continued)

Form 1.3 (Continued)

_____ Review all serial numbers of major equipment.

_____ Unplug all equipment in the room.

_____ Cover all computer equipment.

_____ Store audio and visual equipment.

_____ Place request for additional major end items.

_____ Organize teacher's desk and miscellaneous materials.

_____ Clean desks, chairs, and tables.

IV. Professional Development

_____ Register for summer staff development or college courses for recertification.

_____ Attend summer conferences or seminars relating to special education.

_____ File all conference and article information.

V. Additional Teacher Tasks

_____

_____

_____

_____

_____

_____

_____

_____

_____

_____

_____

_____

Form 1.4   Correspondence Log

Teacher: _____   Month/year: _____

Date: _____

Method: Telephone   Letter   Fax   School note   e-mail

Corresponded with: Mr. Ms. Mrs. _____

In reference to:

_____

_____

_____

_____

Date: _____

Method: Telephone   Letter   Fax   School note   e-mail

Corresponded with: Mr. Ms. Mrs. _____

In reference to:

_____

_____

_____

_____

Date: _____

Method: Telephone   Letter   Fax   School note   e-mail

Corresponded with: Mr. Ms. Mrs. _____

In reference to:

_____

_____

_____

_____

Form 1.5   Student Emergency Information

Student name: _____

Date of birth: _____   Age: _____   Present grade: _____

Student FTE or identification number: _____

Parent or guardian name: _____

Address: _____

Mailing address: _____

Home e-mail address: _____

Home telephone number: _____

Cellular telephone number: _____

Parent or guardian work location: _____

      Telephone number: _____

      Cellular telephone number: _____

      e-mail address: _____

Emergency contact person: _____

      Telephone number: _____

      Cellular telephone number: _____

      e-mail address: _____

Significant medical issues (explain/describe): _____

_____

_____

_____

Medications: _____

Allergies: _____

Wears glasses or contact lenses: Yes or No

Wears hearing aids:	Yes or No	Left ear	Right ear	Both ears
Transportation to school:	Bus	Car	Day care van	Walk
Transportation from school:	Bus	Car	Day care van	Walk

Form 1.6   Noninstructional Classroom Supply Checklist

Teacher: _____   School year: _____

Class/program: _____   Room number: _____

_____ White copy paper (8½ × 11 in.)

_____ Color copy paper (8½ × 11 in.)

     _____ Green   _____ Gray

     _____ Ivory   _____ Pink

     _____ Goldenrod   _____ Lavender

     _____ Salmon   _____ Tan

     _____ Canary   _____ Blue

_____ NCR paper (8½ × 11 in.)
    White/yellow 2-part

_____ NCR paper (8½ × 11 in.)
    White/yellow/pink 3-part

_____ Computer paper (laser or other)

_____ Notebook paper

     _____ Three-ring, 10¼ × 8 in., ruled
     (college or wide rule)

     _____ Wire bound, 11 × 8½ in.

_____ Composition book 10 × 8 in.

_____ Primary practice paper

_____ Notebook binders

     _____ Three-ring, 1-in. diameter

     _____ Three-ring, 1½-in. diameter

     _____ Three-ring, 2-in. diameter

_____ Legal pads, 8½ × 11 in.

     _____ Canary

     _____ White

_____ Teacher plan book

_____ Teacher grade book

_____ E-Z teacher grader

_____ Sentence strips (3 × 24 in.)

_____ Chart tablets

_____ Chart stand

_____ Index cards

_____ Adhesive note pads

     _____ 2 × 3 in.

     _____ 3 × 3 in.

     _____ 3 × 5 in.

_____ Manila file folders

     _____ File folder labels

     _____ File guides A–Z letter

_____ Transparency film

     _____ Acetate writing roll
     _____ Single sheet

_____ Report folders

     _____ 3-fasteners

     _____ Double pockets

_____ Construction paper

     _____ 9 × 12 in. assorted

     _____ 12 × 18 in. assorted

     _____ 18 × 24 in. assorted

_____ Art craft paper

_____ Bulletin board items

     _____ Paper

     _____ Letters

     _____ Border

     _____ Stencils

(Continued)

Form 1.6 (Continued)

_____ Ballpoint pens

    _____ Black ink

    _____ Blue ink

    _____ Red ink

    _____ Green ink

_____ Pencils

    _____ #2 standard

    _____ Red correcting

    _____ Primary

    _____ Mechanical

_____ Permanent markers

    _____ Black

    _____ Blue

    _____ Green

    _____ Red

_____ Highlighter markers

    _____ Set of six highlighters

    _____ Yellow

    _____ Orange

    _____ Blue

_____ Transparency markers

    _____ Black

    _____ Blue

    _____ Red

    _____ Green

_____ Whiteboard dry erase markers

    _____ Set of four colors

    _____ Black

    _____ Blue

_____ Chalk

    _____ White

    _____ Yellow

    _____ Colored

_____ Crayons

_____ Colored markers

_____ Colored pencils

_____ Gem clips

    _____ Small

    _____ Large

    _____ Ideal clamps

_____ Felt stamp pad

    _____ Black

    _____ Red

    _____ Blue

    _____ Green

_____ Glue

    _____ White squeeze

    _____ Glue stick

    _____ Rubber cement

    _____ Paste, jar

_____ Rulers

_____ Meter sticks

_____ Scissors and shears

    _____ Teacher shears

    _____ Student scissors

_____ Stapler (electric or manual)

_____ Staple remover

_____ Thumbtacks

_____ Masking tape

_____ Adhesive tape

_____ Tape dispenser

_____ Paper punchers

     _____ 3-hole punch

     _____ 2-hole punch

     _____ Electric

_____ Computer supplies

     _____ Computer diskettes (formatted/2HD)

     _____ Recordable compact disc (CD-R)

     _____ Mouse pad

     _____ Diskette storage box

     _____ Screen and CD cleaner

     _____ Printer cartridge

     Black, color, or laser

     _____ Surge protector, six outlets

_____ Wite-Out

_____ Quick dry, white

_____ Multipurpose, white

_____ Pen and Ink

_____ Paper towels

_____ Facial tissues

_____ Window cleaner or

other cleaning solution

_____ Disposable latex gloves

_____ Antibacteria soap

_____ First aid kit

_____ Storage containers

_____ File cabinet (locking)

     _____ Four drawer

     _____ Two drawer

Additional list of items to order:

_____   _____

_____   _____

_____   _____

_____   _____

_____   _____

_____   _____

_____   _____

_____   _____

_____   _____

_____   _____

_____   _____

Form 1.7   Instructional Classroom Supply Checklist

Teacher: _____   School year: _____

Class/program: _____   Room number: _____

_____ Curriculum guides for all subject areas

_____ Approved textbooks to support curriculum

_____ Teacher editions for all textbooks

_____ Workbooks and other supporting academic materials

_____ Large-print materials

_____ Books on tape or CD

_____ Supplemental reading material

_____ Computer programs to support academic areas

_____ Visual aids to support academic areas

_____ Manipulatives and models

_____ Technological devices

_____ Audiovisual aids

_____ Telecommunication systems

_____ Additional items:

_____

_____

_____

_____

_____

_____

_____

_____

_____

_____

_____

_____

_____

_____

Form 1.8   Classroom Inventory Checklist

Teacher: _____   School year: _____

Class: _____   Room number: _____

Item	Quantity	Item Description and Serial Number	Condition of Item

Form 1.9   Student Information

Teacher: _____

School: _____

School year: _____

Program: _____

Student Name and Student FTE or ID Number	Student Disability	Current Psychological Date	Current Eligibility Date	IEP Start/ End Dates	Hours Served in Special Education	Hours Served in Regular Education	Medical Concerns and/or Medications	Additional Information

Form 1.10   Present Levels of Performance

Teacher: _____

School: _____

School year: _____

Program: _____

Student Name	Word Recognition Level	Reading Comprehension Level	Written Expression Level	Spelling Level	Math Calculation Level	Math Reasoning Level	Adaptive Behavior Level

Form 1.11   Paraprofessional's Classroom Responsibilities Checklist

Teacher's name: _____   School year: _____

Paraprofessional's name: _____   Program: _____

_____ Assist students in computer lab.   Additional tasks (list):

_____ Assist students in the cafeteria.   _____

_____ Assist students in the media center.   _____

_____ Assist teacher with academic groups.   _____

_____ Assist students using adaptive
equipment or devices.   _____

_____ Assist with the moving of students
to different areas or classes.   _____

_____ Assist students with specific health needs.   _____
(Paraprofessional must be trained by a
licensed health care professional to   _____
assist with specific tasks such as
the suctioning of a tracheotomy tube.)   _____

_____ File students' papers.   _____

_____ Grade students' academic work.   _____

_____ Laminate instructional materials.   _____

_____ Maintain behavior point sheets.   _____

_____ Make copies of instructional materials.   _____

_____ Monitor students during recess.   _____

_____ Monitor/assist students arriving
on school bus or special van.   _____

_____ Organize classroom materials.   _____

_____ Record daily student attendance.   _____

_____ Tutor students in academic areas.   _____

Resource 1.1   Suggestions for Working With a Paraprofessional

Note: In the article "Maximize Paraprofessional Services for Students With Learning Disabilities," Nancy French (2002) emphasizes the need for both general and special education teachers to manage all paraprofessionals in a manner that maximizes their services to students with disabilities. The authors recommend the first-year teacher review the suggestions listed below which were selected from French's original list of twenty before working with his or her assigned paraprofessional.

1. Provide orientation.

2. Determine your program and student needs.

3. Consult with classroom teachers to determine their needs.

4. Create a personalized job assignment for the teaching assistant.

5. Determine the training needs of the teaching assistant.

6. Teach and coach new skills.

7. Give feedback on the performance of new skills.

8. Observe and coach the paraprofessional.

9. Provide work plans.

10. Hold meetings.

Source: Adapted from French, N. K. (2002). Maximize paraprofessional services for students with learning disabilities. *Intervention in School and Clinic, 38*(1), 50–55.

Resource 1.2   Web Sites for Parents and Students

I. Organizations and Resources for Parents

American Association of People With Disabilities Act
www.aapd.com

American Foster Care Resources
www.afcr.com/

Autism Society of America
www.autism-society.org/site/PageServer

Children and Adults With Attention Deficit/Hyperactivity Disorder (CHADD)
www.chadd.org

The Compassionate Friends
www.compassionatefriends.org

Council for Exceptional Children
www.cec.sped.org/home.htm

Council of Independent Colleges
www.cic.edu

Families and Advocates Partnership for Education (FAPE)
www.fape.org

Family and Parenting Resource Center
www.learning4liferesources.com

Family Education
www.familyeducation.com

Family Resource Center on Disabilities
www.frcd.org

Federal Resources for Educational Excellence
www.ed.gov/free

Middle Web
www.middleweb.com

NASP Center: School Dropout Prevention Strategies for Parents
www.naspcenter.org/adol_sdpp.html

National Association for Gifted Children
www.nagc.org

National Association of At-Home Mothers
www.athomemothers.com

National Association of Partners in Education
www.napehq.org

National Coalition for Parent Involvement in Education
www.ncpie.org

National Down Syndrome Society
www.ndss.org

National Military Family Association
www.nmfa.org

National PTA
www.pta.org

National Stepfamily Association
www.stepfam.org

NEA: Help for Parents—Parent Involvement in Education
www.nea.org/parents/research-parents.html

NEA: Parents' Guide to School Improvement
www.nea.org/parents/schoolinvolve.html

Organizations for Parents and Educators of the Gifted
www.d21.k12.il.us/dept_instr/dimensions/organizations.html

Parent Resource Center: At Risk Youth Programs Help for Parents With Troubled Teens
www.parenthelpcenter.org

Parents and Families (Middle School–High School)
www.kde.state.ky.us/KDE/Instructional+Resources/Student+and+Family+Support/Parents+and+Families/c

Parents Count: Resources for Parents of Middle School Students
www.parentscount.net/guidance/detail.cfm?articleID=59

Parents Know
www.parentsknow.com

Parents Without Partners
www.parentswithoutpartners.org

Partnership for a Drug-Free America
www.drugfreeamerica.org

Schwab Foundation for Learning
www.schwablearning.org/index.asp

II. Organizations and Resources for Students

Advocates for Communication Technology for Deaf/Blind People
www.deafblindadvocates.org

American Amputee Foundation
www.okrehab.org/searchfiles/amputations-
SD.html

*American Student Achievement Institute 4-Year High
School Course Plans*
www.asai.indstate.edu/guidingallkids/4yrhscourse
plan.htm

B-CC High School: Student Support Programs
www.mcps.k12.md.us/schools/bcchs/support
.programs.html

Become a Friend of Mapping Your Future
www.isb.ac.th/Content/Detail.asp?ID=299

*EHS Support Groups Help Students Deal
With Life Issues*
www.thisweek-online.com/
2000/november/17support.html

*The English Tutor Online Tutoring for High School
Students*
www.theenglishtutor.com

eSylvan Online Tutoring
www.esylvan.com

Hauppauge Middle School
www.hauppauge.k12.ny.us/new%20web/web2/
Middle%20School/curriculumhs.html

*Health Careers—A Resource Guide
for High School Students*
www.mccg.org/healthcareers/health
careershome.asp

Health Occupations Students of America
www.hosa.org

Learning Styles
www.learning4liferesources.com/
learning_style_1.html

Learning Styles Inventories
www.snow.utoronto.ca/Learn2/introll.html

Links for Math Tutoring
www.ahastars.org/linksmath.html

National FFA Organization
www.ffa.org

Non-Traditional Students Organization
www.studentorgs.swt.edu/ntso

Online Spanish Tutorial
www.LearnPlus.com

Resource Links for Middle School Students
www.nc4h.org/greenlight/kidlinks/links-ms.html

Sibling Support Group
www.sedolfoundation.org/html/Programs.html

Students Against Drunk Driving
www.saddonline.com

Teen Learning Network
www.childadvocate.net

United Nations
www.unol.org

YMCA: Youth Earth Service Corps
www.yesc.org

III. General Resources for Parents and Students

A. College Resource Web Sites

American College Testing
www.act.org

American Universities
www.clas.ufl.edu/CLAS/american-universities.html

Business, Trade, and Technical Schools
www.rwm.org/rwm

College Admissions Process: FishNet
www.jayi.com

College Board
www.collegeboard.org

College Net
www.collegenet.com/

Kaplan Education Center
www.l.kaplan.com

Mapping Your Future
www.mapping-your-future.org/planning

Petersons College Information
www.petersons.com

B. Financial Aid Resources

AESmentor
www.aesmentor.org

(Continued)

Resource 1.2 (Continued)

College Is Possible Campaign
www.collegeispossible.org

*Department of Education, Office of
Postsecondary Education*
www.ed.gov/about/offices/list/ope/index.html

FastWeb
www.fastweb.com

FinAid! Guide to Financial Aid
www.finaid.org

Financial Aid Need Estimator
www.act.org/fane/index.html

Free Application for Federal Student Aid
www.fafsa.ed.gov

PHEAA Creating Access to Education
www.pheaa.org

The Smart Student Guide to Financial Aid
www.finaid.org

C.   Career Resource Web Sites

AESmentor
www.aesmentor.org

America's Career Infonet
www.acinet.org/acinet

Career Experience
www.careerexperience.com

Career Interest Key
www.missouri.edu/~cppcwww/holland.html

Career Magazine
www.careermag.com

*Career Pathways—American Student
Achievement Institute*
www.asai.indstate.edu/guidingallkids/
careerpathways.htm

Career Planning Resource Center
www.learning4liferesources.com/career_
planning_resource_center1.html

Career Resources Center
www.careerresource.com

Careerbuilder
www.careerbuilder.com

Careermag
www.careermag.com

Hot Jobs for the 21st Century
www.dol.gov/dol/wb/public/wb_pubs/hotjobs.htm

Mapping Your Future
www.mapping-your-furture.org

Monster Board
www.monster.com

National Career Development Association
www.ncda.org

NOICC
www.noicc.gov

Occupational Outlook Handbook
www.stats.bls.gov/ocohome.htm

O*NET, Occupational Information Network
www.doleta.gov/programs/onet

Real Game
www.realgame.com

Wall Street Journal Executive Career Site
www.careerjournal.com

What Color Is Your Parachute?
www.jobhuntersbible.com

D.   Alcohol and Substance Abuse

Al-Anon/Al-Ateen
www.al-anon-alateen.org

Publications for Parents
www.ed.gob/pubs/parents

*Safe and Drug-Free Schools Program,
U.S. Department of Education*
www.ed.gov/offices/OESE/SDFS

*Substance Abuse and Mental Health Services
Administration*
www.samhsa.gov

Web of Addictions
www.well.com/user/woa

E. Violence Prevention

Blueprints for Violence Prevention
www.Colorado.EDU/cspv/blueprints

Bullying in Schools
www.ericeece.org/pubs/digest/1997/banks97.html

Coping With School Violence
www.familyeducation.com/topic/front/
0,1156-2179,00.html

Division of Violence Prevention
www.cec.gov/ncipc/dvp/dvp.h.htm

Early Warning, Timely Response: A Guide to Safe Schools
www.athealth.com/consumer/issues/early_
warning.html

National Youth Gang Center
www.iir.com/nygc

School Safety and Legal Rights of Students
www.eric-web.tc.columbia.edu/
digests/dig115.html

Strategies to Reduce School Violence
www.eric-web.tc.columbia.edu/digests/dig115.html

F. Mental Health Resources

*Center for Mental Health Services Knowledge
Exchange Network*
www.mentalhealth.org/index.htm

Child Abuse Prevention Network
www.child-abuse.com

Diagnosis, Research, and Pharmaceutical Information
www.mentalhealth.com

Emotional and Behavior Problems
www.air-dc.org/cecp

Facts for Families
www.aacap.org/factsFam

Federation of Families for Children's Mental Health
www.ffcmh.org

Mental Health Matters
www.mental-health-matters.com

Reporting Child Abuse
www.kidsafe-caps.org/report.html

Stress Management
www.stress.org

Suicide Prevention Action Network
www.spanusa.org

Youth Suicide Prevention
www.sanpedro.com/spcc/suicide

Yellow Ribbon Suicide Prevention Program
www.yellowribbon.org/

Form 1.12 Self-Evaluation Instrument for the Special Education Teacher

INDICATORS	PERFORMANCE LEVELS		
Professional Development/Professional Responsibilities	Exemplary	Satisfactory	Needs Improvement
The special education teacher participates in professional development activities to stay current in his or her field.			
The special education teacher attends district, state, and/or national conferences on a yearly basis.			
The special education teacher has memberships and participates in professional organizations.			
The special education teacher clearly understands state and federal laws regarding students with disabilities.			
The special education teacher maintains current IEPs for all students and reviews students' individual goals and objectives on a regular basis.			
The special education teacher conducts parent conferences in a professional manner.			
The special education teacher maintains a log of all student, parent, faculty, and community contacts.			
The special education teacher conducts needs assessments with parents and students on a yearly basis.			
The special education teacher conducts orientation sessions and workshops with parents and students throughout the school year.			

Form 1.12 (Continued)

INDICATORS	PERFORMANCE LEVELS		
Professional Development/Professional Responsibilities	**Exemplary**	**Satisfactory**	**Needs Improvement**
The special education teacher conducts orientation sessions and workshops with parents and students throughout the school year.			
The special education teacher communicates effectively with general education teachers and other school personnel.			
The special education teacher effectively supervises assigned paraprofessional.			
The special education teacher meets regularly with assigned paraprofessional and provides the individual with the feedback necessary to promote effective practices.			
The special education teacher develops a yearly budget that adequately supports classroom instruction and activities.			
The special education teacher has the skills necessary to effectively use technology in the classroom.			
The special education teacher annually meets with feeder elementary school special education teachers to coordinate the transition of rising students.			

Form 1.12 (Continued)

INDICATORS	PERFORMANCE LEVELS		
Professional Development/Professional Responsibilities	**Exemplary**	**Satisfactory**	**Needs Improvement**
The special education teacher creates and maintains a Web page on the school's Web site.			
The high school special education teacher annually meets with feeder middle special education teachers to coordinate the transition of rising ninth-grade students.			
The special education teacher uses his or her Web page to communicate information to the school community.			
The special education teacher develops a yearly calendar of special classroom events and major school activities (guest speakers, field trips, standardized tests, etc.).			
The special education teacher develops and maintains a professional portfolio.			
The special education teacher maintains a journal highlighting both successful and unsuccessful strategies and activities.			
Additional:			

Form 1.12 (Continued)

		PERFORMANCE LEVELS	
INDICATORS			
Classroom Management Components	**Exemplary**	**Satisfactory**	**Needs Improvement**
The special education teacher ensures that the classroom is clean, comfortable, and conducive to learning for all students.			
The special education teacher ensures that the classroom's color scheme is pleasant and conducive to learning and promotes a positive learning environment.			
The special education teacher ensures that the physical arrangement of the classroom provides a safe and barrier-free environment for all students.			
The special education teacher ensures that the physical arrangement of the classroom is conducive to learning for all students (organization of instructional areas, seating arrangements, independent work areas, etc.).			
The special education teacher ensures that the classroom has aesthetic appeal and promotes a positive learning environment.			
The special education teacher ensures that the classroom furniture and equipment are age appropriate and meet the needs of students with disabilities.			
The special education teacher obtains special or adaptive equipment needed to instruct or assist students (special tables for students in wheelchairs, amplification equipment for hearing-impaired students, Braille note-taker for students with visual impairments, etc.).			

Form 1.12 (Continued)

INDICATORS	PERFORMANCE LEVELS		
Classroom Management Components	**Exemplary**	**Satisfactory**	**Needs Improvement**
The special education teacher ensures that bulletin boards, posters, and other visual aids promote student learning.			
The special education teacher establishes clear classroom behavior expectations and effectively communicates these expectations to students and parents (appropriate classroom rules and consequences).			
The special education teacher develops and implements effective behavior management strategies.			
The special education teacher establishes appropriate classroom policies pertaining to the following: grading system or method, late academic work, class work, homework, makeup work, tardiness, absences, required class materials, reporting student progress, and reporting final grade.			
The special education teacher establishes appropriate classroom procedures pertaining to the following: how students enter and exit the room; excusing students to use the restroom and get water; how and when students can use learning centers, computers, and other classroom equipment; and where students are to place personal items in the classroom.			
The special education teacher develops classroom schedules that include all academic instruction, specialty classes (art, physical education, music, etc.), and/or special services (speech, occupational therapy, etc.).			

Form 1.12 (Continued)

INDICATORS	PERFORMANCE LEVELS		
Instructional Components	**Exemplary**	**Satisfactory**	**Needs Improvement**
The special education teacher reviews the IEP of all students assigned to his or her class before the first day of school and identifies their individual academic goals and objectives that must be addressed during the school year.			
The special education teacher plans for each academic area by completing the following tasks: (a) identifies desired results for each academic area, (b) determines the acceptable evidence of student mastery of identified skills in academic area, and (c) plans learning experiences and instruction that promote student mastery of identified academic skills.			
The special education teacher reviews and selects instructional materials that are appropriate for assigned students.			
The special education teacher plans lessons in advance (at least 1 week).			
The special education teacher includes adaptations in lesson plans to meet the needs of all students.			
The special education teacher prepares a weekly syllabus or homework calendar for students.			
The special education teacher updates Web page weekly and posts all homework assignments and other important class information.			

Form 1.12 (Continued)

INDICATORS	PERFORMANCE LEVELS		
Instructional Components	**Exemplary**	**Satisfactory**	**Needs Improvement**
The special education teacher prepares and obtains all reinforcement materials in advance of the lesson (makes copies, obtains maps and videos, checks technology devices, etc.).			
The special education teacher identifies and posts all weekly instructional objectives in a highly visible location in the classroom.			
The special education teacher plans independent academic activities ("sponges") for periods of time preceding major activities/events, transitions, and/or dismissal. (Sponges are activities that assist students in reviewing or practicing skills previously taught in the classroom.)			
The special education teacher identifies the purpose for each lesson.			
The special education teacher assists students in connecting the purpose of the lessons to their lives.			
The special education teacher reviews prerequisite skills with students.			
The special education teacher gives clear directions, explanations, and relevant examples of content.			
The special education teacher uses a variety of strategies to teach academic material or skills (lecture, collaborative pairs, graphic organizers, etc.).			

Form 1.12 (Continued)

INDICATORS	PERFORMANCE LEVELS		
Instructional Components	**Exemplary**	**Satisfactory**	**Needs Improvement**
The special education teacher models the new skill.			
The special education teacher provides activities that allow all students to respond to ensure mastery of skill.			
The special education teacher uses manipulatives and models to assist students in understanding the skill or concept being taught.			
The special education teacher provides time for guided practice of skill.			
The special education teacher uses activities that promote active listening and responding.			
The special education teacher uses questioning techniques that check the level of students' understanding of content.			
The special education teacher uses appropriate feedback with students responding to questions or attempting to master new skills.			
The special education teacher provides opportunities for students to independently practice new skills.			
The special education teacher uses appropriate closure techniques at the end of the lesson.			

Form 1.12 (Continued)

INDICATORS	PERFORMANCE LEVELS		
Instructional Components	**Exemplary**	**Satisfactory**	**Needs Improvement**
The special education teacher assigns homework to provide students with an opportunity to practice newly acquired skills.			
The special education teacher uses a variety of techniques to evaluate student mastery of the identified objectives of a lesson.			
The special education teacher develops and maintains an academic portfolio for each student.			
Additional:			

Understanding Students With Disabilities

Theories and goals of education don't matter a whit if you do not consider your students to be human beings.

—Lou Ann Walker

Students with disabilities possess unique learning characteristics and bring a spectrum of expectations to the school experience. Olson (2004) noted,

> In the 2002–2003 school year, almost 6 million students ages 6–21 received services under the Individuals with Disabilities Education Act—a number that has increased steadily over the past decade. Those students are classified into 13 different categories under federal law, and the specific needs of each group are very different. (p. 10)

The planning of a quality academic program to effectively meet the needs of a diverse group of students is a major challenge for the beginning teacher. Frequently, first-year special education teachers are placed in positions that differ substantially from their training and area of expertise. Mastropieri (2001) found the following in his research on the challenges encountered by first-year special education teachers:

> Some teachers are assigned positions for which they have not been adequately prepared. Sometimes teachers self-select these positions; other times they are assigned such positions. This issue may actually be increasing over time, for several reasons. First, as school districts move toward more inclusive education models, there is an increased expectation for more special education teachers to work with any student with any disability in any setting. Second, as teacher shortages increase, individuals have more options for teaching position available to them. (p. 72)

In addition, the passage of the No Child Left Behind Act in 2002 presents an additional set of challenges for teachers in the special education profession.

Boehner (2003) notes, "The cornerstone of the No Child Left Behind Act, signed into law by President Bush on January 8, 2002, is improving results for all students, including those with special needs" (p. 1). The new special education teacher must raise standards and plan programs that result in students meeting adequate yearly progress as outlined in the federal law. The teacher's first step toward meeting most challenges is to obtain a clear understanding of each student's individual needs from an educational, physiological, and emotional perspective. The authors recommend that the new teacher spend a tremendous amount of time prior to the start of the school year reviewing and analyzing all information pertaining to the students assigned to his or her caseload. Next, the teacher should schedule time during the first days of school to meet individually with students to begin developing rapport and to obtain students' perceptions of the current special education program or delivery model. Haraway (2002) states, "We as educators sometimes have difficulty listening, really listening to what students and parents say about what they want, what changes they would like us to consider, and what is working well" (p. 60). Finally, the authors highly recommend that the beginning teacher review the disabilities recognized in the Individuals with Disabilities Education Act (IDEA) to have the information necessary to successfully teach in special education delivery models or programs that service students with varying disabilities.

In this chapter, the authors present three strategies designed to facilitate the new teacher's quest to understand students with disabilities. The implementation of these strategies will assist the teacher in developing a quality special education program based on student need, promoting student success in the school setting, and building a positive rapport between teacher and student. The authors have developed forms and surveys that can assist the teacher as he or she strives to understand students with special needs.

STRATEGY 1: REVIEW STUDENT INFORMATION

The reviewing and analyzing of current student information is a task that is tedious and time-consuming; this process, however, is typically the initial step prior to designing and implementing a successful educational program for students. All critical information related to each student is usually contained in a confidential file folder that is secured and maintained by the special education teacher. General student information, such as attendance and transcripts, can be obtained from the student's permanent school record or the school's student information system. The authors have created the Student Folder Checklist and Student Profile form that will guide the new teacher through the review process and the recording of all pertinent student information. All student information is considered highly confidential and may only be shared with individuals who have legal access. The special education teacher should have possession of or access to the following documents for every student on his or her caseload:

- Current Individualized Education Program
- Eligibility document

- Current psychological evaluation
- Classroom performance (general and special class)
- Classroom observations
- School discipline information
- School attendance information
- Student transition plan
- Vision and hearing screening results
- Student transportation information
- Student medical information

Materials or Resources

Form 2.1: Student Folder Checklist

Form 2.2: Student Profile

STRATEGY 2: CONDUCT STUDENT SURVEYS AND INVENTORIES

The first-year special education teacher can use a multitude of strategies to obtain a more comprehensive perspective of each student on his or her caseload. The authors recommend that the teacher use student surveys and inventories as a means of obtaining information and gaining insight into how each student processes information in the academic environment and his or her preferred learning style. These instruments are subjective by design and usually provide the student with the opportunity to communicate to the special education teacher his or her personal thoughts, feelings, and opinions in terms of educational needs. In this section, the authors provide the new teacher with simple surveys and inventories designed to extract essential student information. These instruments make for good independent student activities during the first days of school. The teacher must remember that all collected information must be considered confidential and may only be shared with individuals with approved access.

Materials and Resources

- Form 2.3: Student Academic Inventory

The special education teacher completes the inventory once he or she has reviewed all the student information referred to previously in this chapter. The instructor can use this form when developing classroom modifications for students in inclusive settings.

- Form 2.4: Student Learning Styles Survey

The survey is to be completed by the student on an independent basis. Students who are nonreaders, however, may receive assistance with completing the form from a teacher or peer. The results of the survey will provide the teacher with information regarding the student's preferred learning style.

- Form 2.5: Student Interest Survey

The survey is to be completed by the student on an independent basis. Students who are nonreaders, however, may receive assistance with completing the form from a teacher or peer. The results of the survey will provide the teacher with a greater understanding of the student's personal and school interests.

STRATEGY 3: REVIEW RECOGNIZED DISABILITIES IN IDEA

Special education is constantly evolving and changing in both philosophies and practices as a result of the tremendous amount of research conducted in the field every year. Therefore, it is imperative that teachers be current in the field in their respective areas of expertise. The most prominent changes in practices are the movements toward inclusion of students into the general education classroom and the utilization of the cross-categorical or interrelated special education classrooms. Typically in the inclusion model, students are placed in general education classes on a full-time basis, with a special education teacher providing services to the students in this setting. Often the special education teacher will team teach with the general education teacher, and other times the special teacher will serve as a consultant to these educators. The primary focus of inclusion is the providing of services to students with disabilities in the least restrictive environment. The cross-categorical or interrelated special education classrooms are designed to serve students with different disabilities but similar levels of severity for academic instruction or support. As a result of these current trends, the authors recommend that beginning teachers review current information on all recognized disabilities prior to the start of school and continue to do so throughout the entire year to meet the needs of a diverse group of students with disabilities. Next, the authors provide the reader with the legal definitions for all disabilities that are currently recognized in the regulations of IDEA. The authors strongly suggest that readers refer to their state department of education's definitions for disability categories. In addition, supplemental information is provided for the disabilities that the new special education teacher will most likely encounter. All information is presented in an abbreviated format and intended only as a quick review or reference and not an in-depth study. The authors recommend updating the information provided on a yearly basis.

RECOGNIZED DISABILITIES[1]

SECTION 300.7. Child With a Disability

Autism

Legally Defined: Autism means a developmental disability significantly affecting verbal and nonverbal communication and social interaction, generally evident before age 3, that adversely affects a child's educational performance. Other characteristics often associated with autism are engagement in repetitive activities and stereotyped movements, resistance to environmental change or change in daily routines, and unusual responses to sensory experiences. The

---

[1]SOURCE: U.S. Department of Education (1999).

term does not apply if a child's educational performance is adversely affected primarily because the child has an emotional disturbance, as defined in paragraph (b)(4) of this section.

Typically required eligibility information

Psychological evaluation
Educational evaluation
Communication evaluation
Behavioral observations
Developmental history

Deaf-Blindness

Legally Defined: Deaf-blindness means concomitant hearing and visual impairments, the combination of which causes such severe communication and other developmental and educational needs that they cannot be accommodated in special education programs solely for children with deafness or children with blindness.

Typically required eligibility information

Audiological evaluation
Otological evaluation
Ophthalmological evaluation

Deafness

Legally Defined: Deafness means a hearing impairment that is so severe that the child is impaired in processing linguistic information through hearing, with or without amplification, that adversely affects a child's educational performance.

Typically required eligibility information

Otological evaluation
Audiological evaluation

Emotional Disturbance

Legally Defined:

(i) The term means a condition exhibiting one or more of the following characteristics over a long period of time and to a marked degree that adversely affects a child's educational performance:
  a. An inability to learn that cannot be explained by intellectual, sensory, or health factors
  b. An inability to build or maintain satisfactory interpersonal relationships with peers and teachers
  c. Inappropriate types of behavior or feelings under normal circumstances

    d. A general pervasive mood of unhappiness or depression

    e. A tendency to develop physical symptoms or fears associated with personal or school problems

(ii) The term includes schizophrenia. The term does not apply to children who are socially maladjusted, unless it is determined that they have an emotional disturbance.

Behavioral Disorders

Behavioral disorders and emotional disturbance are generally categorized by whether they are primarily externalizing or internalizing. *Externalizing behaviors* are generally aggressive behaviors expressed outwardly toward other people. *Internalizing behaviors* are those expressed in a more socially withdrawn fashion. The following are examples of behavioral characteristics for each category (Smith & Luckasson, 1992, p. 307):

Externalizing Behaviors	*Internalizing Behaviors*
Hitting other children	Depression
Cursing at a teacher	Withdrawal
Hyperactivity	Fears and phobias
Stealing	Anorexia and bulimia
Arson	Elective mutism

Typically required eligibility information

Psychological evaluation
Educational evaluation
Behavioral observations
Social history

Hearing Impairment

Legally Defined: Hearing impairment means an impairment in hearing, whether permanent or fluctuating, that adversely affects a child's educational performance but that is not included under the definition of deafness in this section (Table 2.1).

Types of hearing loss

1. Conductive hearing losses are due to blockage or damage to the outer or middle ear that prevents sound waves from traveling (being conducted) to the inner ear. Generally, someone with a conductive hearing loss has a mild to moderate disability. Some conductive hearing losses are temporary.

2. Sensorineural hearing loss occurs when there is damage to the inner ear or the auditory nerve (the eighth cranial nerve) and usually cannot be improved medically or surgically. Individuals affected by a sensorineural loss are able to hear different frequencies at different intensity levels; their hearing

Table 2.1 Levels of Hearing Impairment

Hearing Threshold	Ability to Understand Speech
26–40 dB	Difficulty only with faint speech
41–70 dB	Frequent difficulty with normal speech
71–90 dB	Can understand only shouted or amplified speech
91 dB or more	Usually cannot hear any speech

SOURCE: Schildroth & Karchmer (1986, p. 12).

losses are not flat or even. Sensorineural losses are less common in young children than the conductive types (Smith & Luckasson, 1992, p. 385).

3. Congenital hearing losses occur during fetal development or during birth. Most congenital hearing losses are sensorineural and due to either genetic defects or nongenetic factors, such as rubella, diabetes, or an underactive thyroid in the mother during pregnancy (Gearheart, Mullen, & Gearheart, 1993, pp. 234–235).

Assistive listening devices for students with hearing impairments

Hearing aids
Auditory trainers
Audio loop

Typically required eligibility information

Audiological evaluation
Otological evaluation
Educational evaluation

Mental Retardation

Legally Defined: Mental retardation means significantly subaverage general intellectual functioning, existing concurrently with deficits in adaptive behavior and manifested during the developmental period, that adversely affects a child's educational performance.

Etiology: On the basis of current knowledge, approximately 25% of all cases of mental retardation are known to be caused by biological abnormalities. Chromosomal and metabolic disorders, such as Down's syndrome, fragile X syndrome, and phenylketonuria, are the most common disorders manifesting mental retardation. Mental retardation associated with these disorders is usually diagnosed at birth or relatively early in childhood, and the severity is generally moderate to profound.

No specific biological causes can be identified in the remaining 75% of cases. The level of intellectual impairment of a person with no known cause is usually mild, with an IQ between 50 and 70. The diagnosis of mild retardation is not usually made before grade school. In mild mental retardation, a familial pattern is often seen in parents and siblings (Kaplan & Sadock, 1991, p. 686).

Prenatal factors

Rubella (German measles)
Cytomegalic inclusion diseases
Syphilis
AIDS
Complications of pregnancy
Substance abuse

Chromosomal abnormalities

Down's syndrome
Cat-cry (cri-du-chat) syndrome
Fragile X syndrome
Rett's syndrome

Genetic factors

Phenylketonuria
Menkes' disease
Hartnup's disease
Galactosemia
Glycogen storage disease

Acquired childhood diseases

Infection: encephalitis and meningitis
Head trauma
Other issues: cardiac arrest, asphyxia, chronic exposure to lead, and chemotherapy

Intellectual Functioning: Mental retardation is classified according to the degree of intellectual impairment. The AAMD identifies four levels of mental retardation and the IQ range for each (Grossman, 1983):

Retardation Level	Suggested IQ Range
Mild	50–55 to approximately 70
Moderate	35–40 to 50–55
Severe	20–25 to 35–40
Profound	Below 20 or 25

Typically required eligibility information

Psychological evaluation
Educational evaluation
Adaptive behavior evaluation
Relevant medical information

Multiple Disabilities

Legally Defined: Multiple disabilities means concomitant impairments (such as mental retardation-blindness and mental retardation-orthopedic impairment), the combination of which causes such severe educational needs that they cannot be accommodated in the special education programs solely for one of the impairments. The term does not include deaf-blindness.

Orthopedic Impairment

Legally Defined: Orthopedic impairment means a severe orthopedic impairment that adversely affects a child's educational performance. The term includes impairment caused by congenital anomaly (e.g., clubfoot and the absence of a member), impairments caused by disease (e.g., poliomyelitis and bone tuberculosis), and impairments from other causes (e.g., cerebral palsy, amputations, and fractures or burns that cause contractures).

Typically required eligibility information

Medical examination
Educational evaluation
Psychological evaluation

Other Health Impaired

Legally Defined: Other health impaired means having limited strength, vitality, or alertness, including a heightened alertness to environmental stimuli, that results in limited alertness with respect to the educational environment, that

(i) Is due to chronic or acute health problems, such as asthma, attention deficit disorder or attention deficit hyperactivity disorder, diabetes, epilepsy, a heart condition, hemophilia, lead poisoning, leukemia, nephritis, rheumatic fever, and sickle cell anemia; and

(ii) Adversely affects a child's educational performance.

Typically required eligibility information

Medical examination
Educational evaluation
Psychological evaluation

Specific Learning Disability

Legally Defined:

(i) Specific learning disability means a disorder in one or more of the basic psychological processes involved in understanding or in using language, spoken or written, that may manifest itself in an imperfect ability to listen, think, speak, read, write, spell, or to do mathematical calculations, including such conditions as perceptual disabilities, brain injury, minimal brain dysfunction, dyslexia, and developmental aphasia.

(ii) Disorders not included: The term does not include learning problems that are primarily the result of visual, hearing, or motor disabilities; mental retardation; emotional disturbance; or environmental, cultural, or economic disadvantage.

General Information: The authors can find no nationally consistent method for determining whether a student has a specific learning disability. The use of discrepancy scores and formulas is one of the most common approaches for identifying students with specific learning disabilities. In this approach, a standardized intelligence test and standardized achievement test are administered to the student. The results from the intelligence test reveal the student's potential, whereas the achievement test results demonstrate the student's actual academic performance. The student's standard scores on both tests are reviewed and evaluated for significant discrepancies. The following is a list of characteristics of the specific learning disability student:

Mixed dominance

Learning disability in family

Directional confusion

Sequencing problems

No concept of time

Retrieval difficulty

Attention problems

Poor motor control

Disorganized

Reversals

Poor oral reading

Inability to copy

Poor spelling

Trouble with written expression

Leaky memory

Problem with attitude and motivation

Typically required eligibility information

Psychological evaluation
Comprehensive educational evaluation
Analyzed samples of work
Classroom observation
Relevant medical information

Speech or Language Impairment

Legally Defined: Speech or language impairment means a communication disorder, such as stuttering, impaired articulation, language impairment, or a voice impairment, that adversely affects a child's educational performance.

General Information:

Speech disorders: voice, articulation, and fluency

Language disorders: form (phonology, morphology, and syntax), content (semantics), and use (pragmatics)

Typically required eligibility information

> Oral peripheral examination
> Articulation evaluation
> Language evaluation
> Voice evaluation
> Fluency

Traumatic Brain Injury

Legally Defined: Traumatic brain injury means an acquired injury to the brain caused by an external physical force, resulting in total or partial functional disability or psychosocial impairment or both, that adversely affects a child's educational performance. The term applies to open- or closed-head injuries resulting in impairments in one or more areas, such as cognition; language; memory; attention; reasoning; abstract thinking; judgment; problem solving; sensory, perceptual, and motor abilities; psychosocial behavior; physical functions; and information processing and speech. The term does not apply to brain injuries that are congenital or degenerative or to brain injuries induced by birth trauma.

Typically required eligibility information

> A formal report of preinjury functioning
> Medical report
> Psychological evaluation

Visual Impairment

Legally Defined: Visual impairment including blindness means an impairment in vision that, even with correction, adversely affects a child's educational performance. The term includes both partial sight and blindness.

Typically required eligibility information

> Ophthalmologic evaluation
> Educational evaluation

Form 2.1   Student Folder Checklist

Directions: The special education teacher should complete the Student Folder Checklist while simultaneously reviewing each IEP folder in his or her possession. All questions or concerns in reference to the reviewed student information must be noted at the bottom of the form. All information contained on this form is considered highly confidential.

Student name : _____   Date: _____

Student disability: _____   Grade: _____

Information	Yes	No	Comments
Individualized Education Plan (current IEP)			
Eligibility document			
Current psychological evaluation			
Classroom performance			
Classroom observation			
School discipline information			
School attendance information			
Student transition plan			
Vision and hearing screening results			
Transportation information			
Medical information			

Miscellaneous information (list):
  –
  –
  –
  –
  –
  –			

Form 2.2   Student Profile

School year: _____

Student name: _____   Date: _____

Disability: _____   Age: _____   Grade: _____

Directions: The special education teacher should complete a Student Profile form while simultaneously reviewing each student's IEP information.

Student's academic strengths:

_____

_____

_____

Student's academic challenges:

_____

_____

_____

Student's behavior or emotional challenges:

_____

_____

_____

Student's adaptive behavior issues:

_____

_____

_____

Student's transition issues:

_____

_____

_____

Additional information:

_____

_____

_____

_____

Form 2.3   Student Academic Inventory

Directions: The special education teacher should complete a Student Academic Inventory form upon reviewing each student's current IEP, assessments (formal and informal), and classroom performance information.

Student name: _____   Date: _____

Current grade: _____   Age: _____   Disability: _____

How the Student Learns

Sources From Which the Student Can Best Receive, Process, and Retrieve Academic Information	Strengths	Challenges	Instructional Delivery Method	Strengths	Challenges
Textbook			Direct		
Worksheets			Independent study		
Lecture			Peer tutor		
Class discussions			One-on-one teacher assistance		
Audiovisual material			Small group		
Hands-on experiences			Large group		
Observation			Computer-managed		
Other (list): – –			Other (list): – –		

How the Student Responds

Academic Testing Formats on Which the Student Can Best Demonstrate His or Her Degree of Skill Mastery	Strengths	Challenges	Academic Course Assignments	Strengths	Challenges
Written test			Short papers		
Oral test			Worksheets		
Short-answer test			Oral reports		
Essay test			Textbook exercises		
Multiple-choice test			Course projects		
True-false test			Presentations		
Matching test			Vocabulary exercises		
Computation test			Science labs		
Other (list): –			Other (list): –		

Form 2.4   Student Learning Styles Survey

Student name: _____   Date: _____

Class: _____   Grade: _____

Directions: The Student Learning Styles Survey is designed to assist teachers in planning and implementing effective instructional programs. Please answer the questions below to the best of your ability to assist the teacher in obtaining a true understanding of your learning style.

1. Rate the type of tests you prefer on a scale of 1 to 5 (1 = most preferred).

    _____ True/false   _____ Fill-in-the-blank

    _____ Multiple choice   _____ Discussion

    _____ Matching

    _____ Other (list) _____

2. Check the situation in which note taking is most difficult.

    _____ During class lectures   _____ From chalkboard

    _____ From the overhead projector

    _____ Other (what kind) _____

3. Check the situation in which you learn the best.

    _____ Reading material by myself   _____ Class lecture

    _____ Working with a peer   _____ Listening to material on tape

    _____ Other (list/explain) _____

4. Check the environments in which you like to study.

    _____ In my bedroom   _____ A quiet place

    _____ A place with music   _____ In the library

    _____ Other (list/explain) _____

5. When do you study best?

    _____ Morning   _____ Afternoon   _____ Night

6. Check the school subject in which you have the most difficulty.

    _____ Reading   _____ English   _____ Writing

    _____ Math   _____ Science   _____ Social studies

    _____ Other (list) _____

(Continued)

Form 2.4 (Continued)

Student name: _____   Date: _____

Class: _____   Grade: _____

Directions: Please place a check mark in the column beside each statement that applies to you. The comments section may be used to provide further details to help the teacher better understand your needs.

Check   Comments

	I can read tests given in class to myself.	
	I can take notes in class without assistance.	
	I can read class textbooks out loud or to myself.	
	I understand the content in my class textbooks.	
	I can communicate with my teachers.	
	Class material is easier for me to understand when we do labs or other hands-on activities.	
	I maintain an assignment book on a daily basis.	
	I am organized for each class on a daily basis.	
	I have a set study time or schedule and location.	
	I prepare for tests and quizzes in advance.	

Student comments:

_____

_____

_____

_____

_____

_____

_____

_____

_____

Form 2.5   Student Interest Survey

Student name: _____   Date: _____

Directions: The purpose of the Student Interest Survey is to help your teacher get to know you a little better. Please answer all the questions listed in the survey. A teacher, parent, or friend can read the survey to you and assist with the recording of your responses on the form.

1. I like to read about_____

2. In my free time I like to_____

3. I like people who_____

4. My favorite author is_____

5. When I grow up I want to be_____

6. My favorite subject in school is_____

7. My hobby/hobbies are_____

8. I don't like books that_____

9. The place I would like to visit most is_____

10. My favorite vacation was_____

11. The thing I like to do most is_____

12. What I want most in the world is_____

13. I wish_____

14. My favorite song is_____

15. My favorite book is_____

16. My favorite color is_____

17. My favorite food is_____

18. My favorite movie is_____

19. My favorite sport is_____

20. This school year I will_____

Additional information: _____

_____

_____

_____

_____

Placing Students in the Least Restrictive Environment

Coming together is a beginning; keeping together is progress.

—Henry Ford

The term *least restrictive environment* refers to the educational setting for students with disabilities that provides the greatest exposure to the general education curriculum and to an interaction with nondisabled students. The placement process involves the entire Individualized Education Program (IEP) team and must be addressed on a yearly basis. The Individuals with Disabilities Education Act regulations (Section 300.500) mandate that the IEP team make every effort to ensure that students with disabilities are placed with nondisabled students to the maximum extent possible and that removal from this environment is the last resort. During the past several years, the placement of students with disabilities has become an issue that has grown to be a major concern for both special and general education teachers throughout the nation primarily due to the passage of the No Child Left Behind Act in 2000 (NCLB). The specific performance expectations and adequate yearly progress provision in NCLB pertains to all students and has placed a tremendous amount of pressure on school systems to ensure that students with disabilities are progressing at the same rate as nondisabled students. In light of NCLB, school systems are encouraging the placement of students with disabilities into general education classrooms on a full-time basis with special education teachers delivering services to these students through an inclusion model. The beginning teacher must remember that there is a continuum of service delivery options for students with disabilities ranging from the least restrictive environment (general classroom) to the most restrictive environment (hospitals and institutions), and the IEP team must determine the educational environment that best meets the identified needs of the student.

In this chapter, the authors provide the beginning teacher with the information, suggestions, and strategies that have been found critical to the placement of students with disabilities in the least restrictive environment. The chapter is divided into six sections, with each section targeting some aspect of the placement process. The chapter begins with the authors' review of three service delivery models that the beginning teacher is most likely to encounter during his or her first teaching experience and explains the advantages and disadvantages of each model. The authors then outline specific student information for the IEP team to review before making the final placement decision and provide the IEP team with a selection of general classroom modifications and strategies that can be used for students with disabilities in most educational settings. The authors have designed checklists, surveys, supplemental forms, and helpful hints to assist and support the special education teacher and IEP team.

SECTION 1: REVIEW OF SERVICE DELIVERY MODELS

Students with disabilities can receive special education services in a variety of educational settings that range from the general education classroom to a residential care facility. The IEP team determines the most appropriate placement for the student based on his or her educational needs and must document all placement options considered by the team. The information that follows is an overview of three special education service delivery models that the beginning teacher will most likely encounter in his or her new position.

General Class Full-Time

In this delivery model, which is often referred to as inclusion, the student is placed and receives instruction in a general education classroom for most or all of the school day. Typically, students leave the classroom only to receive a related service, such as speech therapy, counseling, or other service as required by the student's IEP. In the inclusion model, the special education teacher can use several methods to provide services to the student. The special education teacher can directly serve the student in the general education classroom or consult, team, or co-teach with the general education teacher. The key to the successful placement of students with disabilities in the general education environment is collaboration, communication, and prior planning.

Advantages[*]

1. Students gain the benefits of being fully included with their peers.

2. All students and teachers learn about diversity and accommodating individual needs.

3. All students benefit from the special education teacher's presence in the classroom.

Disadvantages[*]

1. Some teachers find it difficult to have another teacher in their classrooms.

2. Scheduling time to meet with children in many classes can be difficult.

3. Some children need more support than short visits from the special education teacher can provide.

4. Most teachers do not have enough time to effectively teach to all the needs in the classroom.

Special Class Part-Time

The student is placed and receives instruction in a special education classroom for part of the school day. In this model, which is often referred to as resource or a pullout program, the special education teacher instructs the student in a small group or on an individual basis in the areas of identified need. The student is usually mainstreamed for the remainder of the school day into general education classrooms or activities or both as deemed appropriated by the IEP team. Mainstreaming is the placing of students with disabilities in an educational environment with students who do not have disabilities for a designated period of time during the regular school day. The placement can be of an academic, nonacademic, or extracurricular nature. The special education teacher provides the general education teacher with the necessary modifications for the student to be successful in his or her mainstreamed classes.

Advantages*

1. Students gain the social benefits of being with their peers in a mainstream class.

2. Students receive one-on-one or small group instruction geared to their individual learning needs.

3. All students and teachers learn about diversity and accommodating individual needs.

Disadvantages*

1. Students sometimes miss interesting or important lessons when they are pulled out.

2. Students may feel stigmatized by being pulled out.

3. Scheduling can be difficult.

4. Sometimes students cannot keep up with work of the mainstreamed class.

Special Class Full-Time

Students receive their primary instruction in the special education classroom on a full-time basis. Students in this type of placement are usually mainstreamed into nonacademic classes with nondisabled students.

Advantages*

1. The class size is small.

2. Students get curriculum tailored exactly to their needs.

3. Students spend most of their time with a trained special education teacher.

4. Students who cannot succeed in a mainstream class may do well in this setting.

Disadvantages*

1. Students can be isolated from the rest of the school.

2. Student may feel stigmatized by being in a "special class."

3. Students do not get the social benefits of being included with their peers.

4. It is expensive to have one teacher for a small number of students.

*SOURCE: Used with permission of Flora B. Kupferman, Bureau of Jewish Education of San Francisco, the Peninsula, Marin and Sonoma Counties.

SECTION 2: THE PLACEMENT DECISION

The IEP team must thoroughly review and discuss all current information pertaining to the student before making its final placement decision. The special education teacher should collect and organize the following student information prior to the IEP meeting:

- School attendance information
- Discipline information
- Current levels of academic performance
- Current status of medical condition (if applicable)
- Classroom observation information
- General education teacher summary report or reports

Once a consensus has been reached in terms of the best placement for the student, the IEP team must annotate other placements considered and rejected in the minutes.

Materials and Resources

Form 3.1: Selecting the Least Restrictive Environment Checklist

Form 3.2: Teacher Summary Report

SECTION 3: CLASSROOM ADAPTATIONS

The development of appropriate classroom adaptations is critical when placing students in mainstreamed or inclusive settings. The team must design adaptations based on the student's identified deficit or deficits that will allow the student to progress in the general curriculum. A copy of the agreed-upon classroom adaptations must be given to all teachers who will be working with the student. The authors have included a selection of classroom adaptations at the end of this chapter. The special education teacher can attach this information to the student's individual classroom adaptations and distribute it to the appropriate teachers.

Materials and Resources

Form 3.3: Classifications of Adaptations

Form 3.4: Classroom Adaptations

Form 3.5: Classroom Adaptations Evaluation

Form 3.6: Suggestions for Test Adaptations

Form 3.7: Student's Materials List

SECTION 4: SELECTING TEACHERS FOR STUDENTS IN THE LEAST RESTRICTIVE ENVIRONMENT

Once the IEP team recommends placement, the special education teacher must accomplish a multitude of the tasks that accompany this action. The process of selecting teachers for students placed in the general education environment is extremely difficult for most special education teachers. There are many general education teachers in school systems that work wonderfully with students with special needs, but there are also teachers who simply do not possess the desire, teaching style, or instructional skills that would enable them to meet the needs of students with disabilities in the general education classroom. The ultimate goal of most special educators is to identify colleagues who are amendable to working with students with diversified learning abilities and styles. Most veteran special education teachers have developed a system of selecting appropriate teachers for students with disabilities. New teachers to the field or school system, however, view this task as extremely arduous. The authors suggest three ways in which to begin the selection process. First, the new special education teacher will find that the most reliable sources of information are the veteran special education teachers in his or her school. They will be able to guide and assist the new teacher in his or her selection process. Second, the special teacher can conduct a survey of the school's faculty members. A nonintrusive, generic teacher survey is provided in this chapter. The survey can be easily administered and interpreted. The results of the survey will lay the foundation for selecting appropriate general education teachers for students. Finally, the authors suggest that the new special education teacher seek advice from the principal or other administrative staff. These people usually know the school's faculty and can assist the new teacher in the selection process.

Materials and Resources

Form 3.8a: General Education Teacher Survey Directions

Form 3.8b: General Education Teacher Survey

SECTION 5: MONITORING STUDENTS IN THE GENERAL EDUCATION SETTING

The special education teacher in some fashion must monitor all students placed in general education settings to address academic, behavior, or other problems before they escalate and affect educational performance. The authors have developed four forms that will assist the first-year teacher with the documentation and tracking of student progress.

Materials and Resources

Form 3.9a: Teacher Directions for Completing Student Monitor Form

Form 3.9b: Student Monitor Information

Form 3.10: Student Monitor Results Summary

Form 3.11: Individual Student Progress Report Summary

Form 3.12: Individual Student Final Grade Summary

SECTION 6: TIPS FOR THE GENERAL EDUCATION TEACHER

The authors have selected six disabilities recognized in the current regulations of the Individuals with Disabilities Education Act and provide recommended educational strategies for each disability. Both special and general education teachers can use the strategies listed in this section.

Tips for Teachers of Students With Specific Learning Disabilities

1. The student should sit in a location that is free from distractions and in close proximity to the instructor.

2. Write all homework or class assignments on the board.

3. Use peer tutoring or peer helping. The peer tutor or helper can assist the student in the following manner:
   a. Making certain the student understands directions of assignments
   b. Reading important directions and essential material to them
   c. Drilling them orally on what they need to know
   d. Orally summarizing important textbook passages for the student
   e. Working with them in joint assignments
   f. Critiquing the student's work and making suggestions for improvement

4. Use a multisensory approach to instruction when possible.

5. Conference with the student as much as possible to verify that the student understands the course material and all instructions.

6. Give students several alternatives to obtain and report information: tapes, interviews, reading, experience, making something, etc.

7. Give students shortened assignments.

8. Set up a specific homework schedule or test schedule or both so the student will know what to expect.

9. Allow the student to underline or highlight in his or her textbook.

10. Encourage the student to use flashcards for vocabulary word review.

11. Give positive reinforcement as often as possible.

12. Modify tests or quizzes according to the student's IEP.

Tips for Teachers of Students With Behavioral Disorders

1. Establish clear rules for the class and post in highly visible location.

2. Speech rules are most effective when they are
   a. Few in number
   b. Relatively short
   c. Stated positively (e.g., "Work quietly" rather than "Do not make noise")
   d. Regularly reviewed with students (Rizzo & Zabel, 1988, p. 220)

3. Reinforce individual students when they follow the rules.

4. Ignore inappropriate behavior when possible.

5. Ensure that the consequences for not following the rules are fair, realistic, and appropriate for the offense.

6. Develop a "safe plan" for times when the student feels as though he or she is about to lose control (e.g., may go to see the school counselor or stand in the hallway).

7. Provide an environment that is structured.

8. Post the class schedule or routine. The teacher should inform the student in advance of changes to the class schedule.

9. Contact the student's parents to report both positive and negative information equally.

10. Maintain accurate records on classroom behavior. Contact parents if the student exhibits significant and drastic changes in behavior.

11. Frequently praise the student.

12. Assign the student room responsibilities that will promote self-confidence.

Tips for Teachers of Other Health-Impaired Students[1]

1. Be alert to signs of fatigue in the child.

2. Find teaching materials that can be adapted to the physical needs of the student.

3. Use teaching materials and activities that are appropriate for the age of the student.

4. Make sure that all areas of the room and school are accessible.

5. Make sure materials, projects, or leisure activities are within the student's reach.

6. Encourage personal privacy when assisting the student with hygiene.

7. Include activities each day that the student can accomplish from a wheelchair.

8. Lift only as much weight as you can.

9. Post emergency instructions and telephone numbers.

[1]SOURCE: Smith and Luckasson (1992, p. 452).

Tips for Teachers of Students With Attention Deficit Disorder or Attention Deficit Hyperactivity Disorder

1. Preferential seating: The teacher should design a seating chart that will place the attention deficit disorder/attention deficit hyperactivity disorder student in close proximity of instruction and away from areas of distraction.

2. Classroom rules and consequences should be clear and concise and placed in a highly visible area.

3. Present clear, specific, and simple directions in both written and oral form.

4. Post the classroom schedule or routine.

5. Avoid heavy doses of seatwork.

6. Provide an area in the room where the student can retreat when he or she is having a difficult time staying focused or controlling his or her activity level. Study carrels work well for elementary students.

7. Provide the student with concrete activities and examples to demonstrate abstract concepts. Use hands-on activities or manipulatives or both when possible.

8. Use visual and verbal prompts and cues to maintain on-task behavior.

9. Provide the student with opportunities to move around the room—running errands, helping in the classroom, handing out papers, cleaning the board, etc.

10. Positively reinforce appropriate behavior immediately.

11. Provide the student with a particular time frame for assignment completion. Assignments should be broken down into smaller pieces.

12. Allow an extended amount of time for assignment completion.

13. Use medium-intensity lighting.

Tips for Teachers of Students With Hearing Impairments

Mild to Moderate Hearing Losses

1. Talk facing the student.

2. The student should sit close to the teacher or in the direction of instruction.

3. The teacher should not stand in glaring light or with his or her back to an open window because this interferes with effective lipreading.

4. If the student appears to be inattentive or not following your instruction, make certain that the student's hearing aid is turned on.

5. The student should use complete but brief sentences during instruction.

6. Reduce the background noise as much as possible.

7. Articulate clearly, but do not talk louder unless you have an unusually soft voice.

8. Make certain you have the student's attention before talking or starting a lesson.

9. Speak normally. Do not overenunciate words, speak louder than usual, or have forced facial expressions.

10. Do not chew gum or cover your mouth when talking.

11. Use visual aids whenever possible; an overhead projector is preferable to a blackboard.

12. The teacher should familiarize the student with new vocabulary prior to introducing the new topic in class.

13. Repeat and restate information by paraphrasing.

Tips for Teachers of Students With Speech or Language Impairments or Both[2]

1. Be alert to the presence of speech or language disorders.

2. Refer children suspected of having a communicative disorder to a speech and language pathologist (SLP).

---

[2]SOURCE: Smith and Luckasson (1992, p. 191).

3. Remember that children with speech or language disorders have difficulty communicating with others.

4. Work with the SLP to integrate appropriate language development activities in all academic instruction.

5. Incorporate activities in class that allow children to practice skills mastered in therapy.

6. Always consider the developmental stage of the child suspected of having a communicative disorder before making a referral.

7. Create a supportive environment in which children are encouraged to communicate with each other.

8. Create a section of the classroom where the physical environment— perhaps a large, round table—encourages sharing and discussion.

9. Provide opportunities for children to feel free to exchange ideas and discuss what they are learning in different subjects.

10. Arrange for activities in which children use oral language for different purposes (e.g., making a speech and leading a discussion) with different audiences (e.g., classmates and children in different classes).

11. Build self-confidence in all children, particularly those with communicative disorders.

Form 3.1   Selecting the Least Restrictive Environment Checklist

Student name: _____   Date: _____

Team signatures:

_____   _____

_____   _____

_____   _____

Directions: Read each statement below and check only the statement or statements that apply to the student at the present time. Complete the summary at the bottom of the page based on the responses.

_____ The student's educational needs can be met in the general education classroom with mild modifications to the instructional program.

_____ The general education environment will not impede the learning of the student.

_____ The student possesses the foundation or prerequisite academic skills necessary to be successful in the general classroom.

_____ The student possesses the social skills necessary to foster healthy peer relationships.

_____ The student demonstrates frequent on-task behavior.

_____ The student demonstrates adequate study skills.

_____ The student can follow classroom rules and understands the consequence of misbehavior.

_____ The student possesses a desire to be with students who do not have disabilities.

_____ The student's behavior in the general education classroom will not impair the education of students who do not have disabilities.

SUMMARY:

_____ The student would benefit from receiving his or her primary academic instruction in the general education classroom for the areas circled below:

Circle recommendations: Reading   English   Math   Science   Social studies

Other: _____

_____ The student would benefit from participating in nonacademic activities in the general education classroom for the activities circled below:

Circle recommendations: Recess   Lunch   Assemblies   Clubs   Music   Art   Computer

Other: _____

_____ The student would not benefit from an inclusive setting at this time.

Form 3.2   Teacher Summary Report

Student name: _____   Date: _____

Teacher: _____

Class: _____   Period: _____

Directions: Please describe in detail how the student interacts and performs in your classroom on an average basis. The information will be used by the IEP team to facilitate the decision-making process in terms of appropriate inclusive settings for the student.

_____

_____

_____

_____

_____

_____

_____

_____

_____

_____

_____

_____

_____

_____

Please return to: _____

Due date: _____

Form 3.3   Classifications of Adaptations

Accommodations

Adams (as cited in Polloway, Epstein, & Bursuck, 2003) defined accommodations as the changes in input and output processes in teaching and assessment, such as the format of instructional presentations and test practice and/or preparation activities, the setting for a test, the scheduling or timing of instruction or assessment, and the response format called for in an assessment procedure.

Modifications

"The concept of modifications refers to changes in content and/or standards. In curricular areas, modifications could involve changes in content and/or skill expectations for different groups of students. A key testing modification would be limiting the amount of material upon which a student is evaluated" (Polloway et al., 2003, p. 190).

Form 3.4   Classroom Adaptations

Student name: _____   Date: _____

Grade: _____   Subject: _____   Period: _____

General education teacher: _____

Special education teacher: _____

Note: The classroom adaptations checked below should be implemented for the student to experience success in his or her general education class or classes. The modifications selected are in compliance with the student's IEP. In addition, the modifications are appropriate based on the student's identified and documented learning needs.

_____ Preferential seating

_____ Modified tests (circle):
Oral tests
Open-book tests
Shortened tests
Eliminate choices on multiple-choice tests.
Allow extended time to complete tests.
Tests may be read to student.

_____ Student may leave class for assistance from his or her special education teacher. (This must be arranged in advance.)

_____ Modified assignments (circle):
Shortened assignments (fewer math problems, fewer pages to read, etc.)
Extended time for assignment completion
Allow student to use several alternatives to obtain information for reports: tapes, interviews, reading, experience, etc.

_____ Assignment book

_____ Mark student's correct and acceptable work only.

_____ Note-taking assistance

_____ Recognize and give credit for student's oral participation in class.

_____ Use cross-age tutoring.

_____ Avoid placing student under pressure of time or competition.

_____ Written assignments may be taped.

_____ Student may use cursive or manuscript writing.

_____ Give directions verbally and in written form.

_____ Use a behavior point system.

_____ Quietly repeat directions to student.

_____ Taped text or lectures.

_____ Praise or reward student for appropriate behavior.

_____ Special equipment needed or other recommended modifications (list):

Form 3.5   Classroom Adaptations Evaluation

Student name: _____   Date: _____

General education class: _____   Period: _____

General education teacher: _____

Directions: List the adaptations that were implemented in the general education environment to meet the needs of the inclusive student. Record and discuss the results of each, and use the comments section to note all pertinent information.

Start Date	End Date	Adaptations	Results	Comments

Form 3.6   Suggestions for Test Adaptations

Test Description	Required Student Skills, Arlington County Public Schools—1999	Suggested Test Modifications
Computation	Possess content knowledge Demonstrate good organizational skills Read at test vocabulary level Possess legible penmanship Possess the visual perceptual skills necessary to read and place the numbers in the correct order and space	Extended time for completion Use graphing paper or ruler Use calculator
Essay/short answer	Possess content knowledge Demonstrate good memory skills Possess the ability to process Read at test vocabulary level a large quantity of material Possess an excellent vocabulary Possess good writing skills Demonstrate legible penmanship, good organizational and conceptual skills	Extended time for completion Read test to student Rephrase/restate question Use word processing program (computer)
Fill-in-the-blank	Possess content knowledge Read at test vocabulary level Possess good writing skills Possess good memory skills Possess the ability to copy the answers	Extended time for completion Provide a word bank Read test to student
Matching	Possess content knowledge Read at test vocabulary level Possess ability to visually track Possess ability to discriminate figure test items from ground	Extended time for completion Read test to student Divide test into sections and color code each section and possible choices
Multiple choice	Possess content knowledge Read at test vocabulary level Possess the ability to copy the answers or have the necessary visual perceptual skills to circle a letter/number or to transfer that letter/number to a separate paper	Extended time for completion Eliminate a possible answer (choice) for each question Read test to student
True/false	Possess content knowledge Possess legible penmanship Possess the ability to discriminate Read at test vocabulary level inclusive vocabulary from exclusive vocabulary	Extended time for completion Read test to student Allow student to highlight key words: "all" and "never"

Form 3.7   Student's Materials List

Student name: _____   Date: _____

The items checked below are recommended for your general education class or classes:

_____ Three-ring binder with subject dividers   Additional materials:

_____ Trapper Keeper   _____

_____ Pencils   _____

_____ Ink pens   _____

_____ Assignment book   _____

_____ Paper   _____

_____ Pocket folders   _____

_____ Book bag   _____

_____ Calculator   _____

_____ Math compass   _____

_____ Graph paper   _____

_____ Glue   _____

_____ Scissors   _____

_____ Crayons   _____

_____ Color markers   _____

_____ Colored pencils   _____

_____ Index cards   _____

_____ Spiral notebook   _____

Parent signature: _____

Date: _____

Form 3.8a   General Education Teacher Survey Directions

Directions: The attached survey is designed to facilitate the process of selecting general education teachers for students with disabilities. The results of the survey will assist the special education teacher in his or her effort to match teaching styles with students' learning styles. Please read each question carefully and place a check mark by the statements that accurately describe your teaching style, techniques, and philosophy. The results of the survey are confidential and will be maintained in a locked file cabinet for security.

Please return to: _____

Due date: _____

Form 3.8b   General Education Teacher Survey

Date: _____

Teacher: _____   Grade: _____

Subject: _____

1. _____ The students have assigned seats and I maintain a seating chart.
2. _____ The students are allowed to sit in a location of their choice.
3. _____ The students are required to maintain an organized notebook.
4. _____ The students are given a list of required materials for the class.
5. _____ Classroom rules and consequences are posted in a highly visible location and have been discussed in detail with the students.
6. _____ The students are required to maintain an assignment book.
7. _____ I encourage the students to write down all assignments.
8. _____ I write all assignments on an assignment board or in a highly visible location.
9. _____ I give a weekly or unit syllabus to all students.
10. _____ Graded papers are returned immediately to the students.
11. _____ Graded papers are sent home once a week and a parent signature is required before returning papers to school.
12. _____ Students are frequently divided into cooperative learning groups for various classroom activities.
13. _____ Students are placed in groups only for the purpose of lab activities or major class projects.
14. _____ Students are required to take notes on a daily basis.
15. _____ Students are encouraged to take notes; however, I provide handouts that cover the key points of a section, chapter, or unit.
16. _____ I use a lecture format as a primary means of instruction.
17. _____ I use a combination of lecture and discussion as a primary means of instruction.
18. _____ I use a combination of lecture, discussion, and hands-on activities as a primary format of instruction.
19. _____ My tests are strictly objective: multiple choice, fill-in-the-blank, or matching.
20. _____ My tests are strictly subjective: essay.
21. _____ My tests are a combination of objective and subjective.
22. _____ I provide opportunities for remediation.
23. _____ Students are given weekly progress reports.
24. _____ Students are given progress reports or report cards as directed by the school system.
25. _____ Parents are notified when a student is not performing to his or her potential.
26. _____ I use technology in the classroom.
27. _____ I modify test or instructional materials to meet the needs of the students.
28. _____ I enjoy working with students from all backgrounds.
29. _____ I am firm and consistent with the classroom discipline policy.
30. _____ I am organized and structured in my approach to teaching.

Form 3.9a   Teacher Directions for Completing Student Monitor Form

The special education teacher should periodically monitor all students placed in inclusion or mainstreamed settings to address problems before they escalate and affect student performance. One of the most time-efficient methods of monitoring students is by way of a checklist. The authors have developed a monitor checklist for general education teachers. This checklist can be quickly completed by the teachers and provides a total view of student performance in the general education classroom. Please review the following directions before distributing the Student Monitor Information form to teachers who instruct students with disabilities.

Directions:

1. Complete the top portion of the monitor form and distribute to each teacher of the inclusive student.

2. Monitor forms should be given to each teacher at the minimum of every 3 weeks or between each official school reporting period.

3. Explain to each teacher that the information completed on the form will be shared with the student and the parent when appropriate.

4. Upon receiving a monitor form that indicates areas of concerns, consult with the teacher as soon as possible.

5. Arrange a conference as soon as possible when concerns are of significant magnitude.

6. Special education teachers should maintain a folder of all monitor forms for documentation purposes.

7. Monitor forms should be reviewed at the annual Individualized Education Program team meeting.

Form 3.9b   Student Monitor Information

Student: _____   Date: _____

Subject: _____   Teacher: _____

Note: The information recorded on this monitor form will be shared with the student and his or her parents/guardians when appropriate and filed for documentation.

Class participation: Pass: _____   Fail: _____

Class or daily work: Pass: _____   Fail: _____

Homework: Pass: _____   Fail: _____

Quiz grades: Pass: _____   Fail: _____

Test grades: Pass: _____   Fail: _____

On-task behavior: Good: _____ Fair: ___ Poor: _____

Tardy/absent: T: _____   AB: _____

Overall performance: Pass: _____   Fail: _____

Teacher request conference: Yes: _____   No: _____

Teacher concerns:

_____

_____

_____

Return form to: _____

Due date: _____

Form 3.10   Student Monitor Results Summary

Student name: _____   Report date: _____

Report period: _____

Note: This form is to be used as a summary for the Student Monitor Information form (Form 3.9). Review each student's completed monitor forms and place check marks in the problem areas for each subject. The summary form is a quick reference of a student's progress in an inclusion or mainstreamed setting.

Subject	Class Participation	Daily Class Work	Daily Homework	Quiz Grades	Test Grades	On-Task Behavior	Overall Performance	Tardy	Absent

Form 3.11   Individual Student Progress Report Summary

School year: _____

Reporting period: _____

Directions: The special education teacher should record all grades that his or her students received in their inclusion or mainstreamed classes during the progress report time period. Schools usually issue a formal progress report halfway through each reporting period. The authors strongly recommend that the teacher highlight all subjects in which students received a grade of "D" or "F."

Student Name	Language Arts	Mathematics	Science	Social Studies	Physical Education	Elective or Exploratory

Form 3.12   Individual Student Final Grade Summary

Student name: _____

Semester: _____   School year: _____

Academic Subject	First Reporting Period Average	Second Reporting Period Average	Third Reporting Period Average	Semester Exam Grade	Days Absent	Conduct Average	Teacher's Comment

Additional information:

_____

_____

_____

_____

Managing the Classroom

4

In an effective classroom students should not only know what they are doing, they should also know why and how.

—Harry Wong

Classroom management can be defined as "a complex task consisting of planning lessons, providing safe environments, teaching students, and perhaps the most daunting task of all, appropriately responding to student behavior problems" (Backes & Ellis, 2003, p. 23). An effective classroom management plan is the key to building a strong instructional program and plays a critical role in the learning process for all students. Marzano and Marzano (2003) found the following:

> Research has shown us that teachers' actions in their classrooms have twice the impact on student achievement as do school policies regarding curriculum, assessment, staff collegiality, and community involvement. We also know that one of the classroom teacher's most important jobs is managing the classroom. (p. 6)

The authors recognize that a tremendous amount of diversity exists among special education programs and delivery models; the beginning teacher, however, must have a working knowledge of the basic components of an effective classroom management plan regardless of his or her current position. The teacher should be able to apply this knowledge to a variety of educational settings, including the general education classroom. The components of a comprehensive classroom management plan that promotes student learning are as follows:

- The physical arrangement and décor of the classroom are inviting and conducive to learning.
- The classroom climate is supportive and reflects a sense of mutual respect between teacher and students.

- The teacher communicates the expectations for students' academic performances and behaviors in the classroom.
- The classroom's policies and procedures clearly regulate all activities.

The task of developing a classroom management plan must be accomplished prior to the start of the school year, and the plan must be in place on the first day of school to promote a positive learning environment and prevent total chaos. The plan should reflect the basic educational philosophy of the teacher, be appropriate for the student population, and be approved by the school's principal. The authors recommend that the beginning teacher enlist the assistance of a veteran teacher, possibly a mentor, when developing his or her first classroom management system. Veteran teachers are great sources of information and usually have insight into "what works" based on their own experiences.

In the following sections, the authors present a six-step process that is designed to assist the first-year teacher in developing a comprehensive and effective plan. The authors identify and present the critical components of an effective classroom plan and provide the beginning teacher with strategies designed to support each component. The process includes requiring the teacher to review his or her school's policies pertaining to teachers and students before developing and implementing his or her first classroom management plan and evaluating the success of the plan at the end of the school year. The authors provide the reader with supplemental checklists, forms, and information that will assist and support the new special education teacher in this endeavor.

STEP 1: REVIEW THE SCHOOL'S POLICIES AND PROCEDURES PERTAINING TO STUDENT AND TEACHER EXPECTATIONS

The teacher's management plan must fit within the framework of his or her assigned school's policies. Most schools have faculty and student handbooks that contain a wealth of information and are a quick reference of school expectations. The teacher should obtain a copy of the student handbook and read all policies that relate to academic requirements, dress code, rules and consequences, and other miscellaneous information that should be incorporated into his or her plan. The authors recommend that the beginning teacher, once hired for his or her current position, read and possibly memorize the faculty handbook. The faculty handbook is the compass that enables the new teacher to chart a course toward an appropriate classroom management plan.

STEP 2: ENSURE THAT THE PHYSICAL ARRANGEMENT AND DÉCOR OF THE CLASSROOM ARE INVITING AND CONDUCIVE TO LEARNING

The teacher must consider several environmental factors when designing his or her classroom. The classroom's physical arrangement, color scheme, bulletin board designs, temperature, lighting, and space are all factors that impact student learning. Students' desks or tables should be arranged in a manner that allows the teacher to move among students with ease and promotes student-centered instruction. The classroom's walls should be light in hue to provide a pleasant backdrop for instruction. Bulletin boards can typically be found inside or outside the classroom or both and are excellent tools for reinforcing academic skills, showcasing students' best works, and reinforcing positive student behaviors. The teacher should select and use contrasting colors when decorating class bulletin boards. Colors that contrast one another on the color wheel are stimulating in nature (e.g., blue and orange), whereas colors that are next to one another on the color wheel are calming in nature (e.g., peach and rose). The authors suggest that teachers enlist the help of their students in designing and constructing the bulletin boards in the classroom. The room temperature and lighting also impact student learning. The room temperature and lighting must be at a level that does not impede student performance. In terms of space, studies (Berdine & Cegelka [1980] and Mercer & Mercer [1998] as cited in Lewis & Doorlag, 2003) found that classroom space should be divided into performance areas or zones to accommodate routine activities and tasks. The teacher should modify or adapt all classroom designs to accommodate the needs of students with disabilities.

Materials or Resources

Resource 4.1: Tips for Classroom Arrangement

Resource 4.2: Bulletin Board Guidelines and Information

STEP 3: ENSURE THAT THE CLASSROOM CLIMATE IS SUPPORTIVE AND REFLECTS A SENSE OF MUTUAL RESPECT BETWEEN TEACHER AND STUDENTS

The classroom climate must be supportive and reflect a sense of mutual respect among all stakeholders to foster the learning process. Marzano and Marzano (2003) conducted studies on the quality of teacher-student relationships and found that "teachers who had high-quality relationships with their students had 31% fewer discipline problems, rule violations, and related problems over a year's time than did teachers who did not have the same relationship" (p. 6). The purpose of establishing quality relationships with students is not only to prevent or decrease discipline issues but also to convey to students that the classroom is a safe place to try newly acquired skills. In addition, Backes and Ellis (2003) state, "A key element in assuming leadership of a classroom is to convey to students that they are important and that the teacher is confident that they can master the content" (p. 23). There will be occasions when conflict in the classroom will arise and threaten to diminish the supportive climate and damage relationships among members of the classroom. Teachers must address and resolve conflicts in a timely manner. The teacher can use individual student conferences when the conflict involves only a few students; the authors have found, however, that holding a class meeting is extremely effective when the conflict involves a large group of students. Class meetings allow students to discuss problem areas without ridicule and develop solutions to resolve conflicts. The teacher is the facilitator and lays the ground rules for all meetings at the beginning of the school year. The teacher may also have to address the bullying and harassment of students sometime during the school year. These are major issues that can lead to serious consequences if not addressed by the teacher expeditiously. Many school systems have specific policies and procedures regarding these areas, and the teacher must familiarize himself or herself with this information. According to McNamara (as cited in Salend, 2001), "You may need to deal with bullying or peer harassment, which may take the form of extorting lunch money, taunting, name-calling, spreading false rumors, and using verbal and physical threats" (p. 258). The authors suggest that the beginning teacher use a variety of methods and resources to convey to students that they are valuable members of the classroom.

STEP 4: COMMUNICATE ALL EXPECTATIONS FOR STUDENTS' ACADEMIC PERFORMANCES AND BEHAVIORS IN THE CLASSROOM

The authors advise the new teacher to thoroughly explain classroom expectations for academic performance and behavior with students as soon as possible. "Communication, both nonverbal and verbal, is the 'stuff' that initiates, builds, maintains, and destroys relationships" (Miller, Wackman, Nunnally, & Miller, 1988, p. 9). Teachers must "raise the bar" in terms of setting high expectations for the academic performance of all students. The teacher must clearly define acceptable and unacceptable student work and challenge students to meet his or her expectations. Teachers must celebrate students' successes and provide encouragement when a student's mastery of learning objectives is not achieved.

The establishment and implementation of classroom rules and consequences and the recognition of students for following the rules are essential to maintaining a sense of order in the classroom. The new teacher must select an approach to classroom discipline that does not conflict with his or her educational philosophy and fits the needs of the educational program. A large majority of both general and special education teachers use some aspect of the assertive discipline approach developed by Lee and Marlene Canter. The establishment of rules and consequences and reinforcement of positive behavior are both a part of the assertive discipline model. The authors have found that classroom rules seem to be more meaningful to students when they are allowed to assist in selecting or developing the rules. Another discipline model that is often used by special education teachers is the behavior analysis model: "The key to this model is the use of reinforcers, both positive and negative, to obtain desired behavior and to extinguish inappropriate behavior" (Koorland, 1995, p. 149). The authors have found this approach to be not only effective in changing the inappropriate behavior of students with disabilities but also extremely successful with general education students. The authors recommend that the first-year special education teacher develop a classroom discipline plan prior to the start of the school year. Suggestions for developing rules and consequences and behavior management plans are included at the end of the chapter. The new teacher should obtain approval from the school principal for all classroom discipline plans and behavior modification strategies prior to implementation.

Materials or Resources

Resource 4.3: Tips for Communicating With Students and Parents

Resource 4.4: Tips for Developing Classroom Rules and Consequences

Resource 4.5: Tips for Developing Behavior Modification Plans

Form 4.1: Daily Point System

Form 4.2: Behavior Contract

Form 4.3: Student Progress Report

STEP 5: DEVELOP CLASSROOM POLICIES AND PROCEDURES THAT CLEARLY REGULATE ALL ACTIVITIES

According to Harry Wong (1991), "Effective teachers spend a good deal of time the first weeks of the school year introducing, teaching, modeling, and practicing procedures until they become routines" (p. 1). The establishing of policies and procedures is extremely important to the basic operation of the special education classroom. The new teacher must understand the difference between the two terms before developing his or her plan of action. Classroom procedures are designated methods for completing certain class activities or tasks. The teacher can think of classroom procedures as the way to "conduct business" in the classroom. Classroom policies are a set of guiding principles or courses of action. The authors recommend that the teacher review the Classroom Policies and Procedures Checklist at the end of the chapter and select the activities or issues that apply to his or her current teaching situation. The authors suggest that the teacher add items as needed at the end of the list.

Materials or Resources

Form 4.4: Classroom Policies and Procedures Checklist

STEP 6: EVALUATE THE OVERALL EFFECTIVENESS OF THE CLASSROOM MANAGEMENT PLAN

The authors strongly encourage the beginning teacher to evaluate his or her classroom management plan at the end of the school year. The evaluation process can be a matter of self-reflection or may also include an informal survey of students and parents. The authors have found that the evaluation is more meaningful when all stakeholders have been included in the process. The authors have provided a sample evaluation form at the end of the chapter. The form is basic by design and may be revised to best meet the needs of the teacher and older students.

Materials or Resources

Form 4.5: Classroom Management Plan Evaluation

Resource 4.1 Tips for Classroom Arrangement

- Ensure that the classroom is barrier free and safe for students.

- Designate specific areas of the classroom for specific activities:

  Main instruction area

  Small-group instruction area

  Learning centers area

  Computer or technology area

  Free reading area

  Reference book area

  Teacher instructional materials area

  Student materials area

  Independent study area

  Listening center area

  Teacher storage area

- Place teacher's desk in the best location to monitor students and the location least likely to interfere with instruction.

- Place paraprofessional's desk area in the best area to assist students.

- Arrange students' desks in a manner that is conducive to student-centered instruction.

Resource 4.2   Bulletin Board Guidelines and Information

- Bulletin boards can be used for a variety of purposes:

  Displaying student work (neatly)

  Displaying class schedule

  Displaying monthly calendar

  Posting of school news

  Extension of instructional unit or theme

  Aiding in instruction/reinforcing skills

  Posting notices

  Decorating the classroom

  Displaying word of the day

- Commercial or teacher-made materials can be used.

- Materials should be laminated for durability.

- Make titles for bulletin boards to explain themes or purposes.

- Use contrasting colors.

- Bulletin boards are appropriate for all age-groups.

- Designate a storage place for all bulletin board materials.

Resource 4.3   Tips for Communicating With Students and Parents

- Certificates and awards

- Class meetings

- Daily progress report

- Display students' best work on a special bulletin board

- Individual conference with student

- Positive notes to parents or guardians

- Positive notes to students

- Positive sticker on a good paper

- Positive telephone calls or e-mails to parents or guardians

- Recognize acts of kindness toward other classmates

- Special class privileges

- Tangible rewards

- Teacher-student conferences

- Verbal praise

- Weekly progress report

NOTE: Canter and Canter (1995) state that "positive recognition will motivate students to follow rules that the teacher creates" (p. 255).

Resource 4.4 Tips for Developing Classroom Rules and Consequences

Classroom Rules

- Rules should be few in number: One to five are plenty.

- Rules should be positively stated ("Work quietly" vs. "Don't talk").

- Rules should be appropriate for the student's age and identified area of challenge.

- Rules should fall within the school guidelines (include school rules).

Classroom Consequences

- Consequences must be appropriate for infraction.

- Consequences must be enforced consistently and as immediately as possible.

- "Consequences should be listed in a discipline hierarchy" (Canter & Canter, 1995, p. 257)—for example, warning, first offense, and second offense.

Resource 4.5   Tips for Developing Behavior Modification Plans

- Clearly identify the target behavior (the behavior to be changed).

- Collect information on when the behavior occurs and under what conditions.

- Write a behavioral objective.

- Implement reinforcement and chart effectiveness.

- Vary the reinforcement schedule and chart results.

- Stop the reinforcement and evaluate student behavior.

Form 4.1   Daily Point System

Week of: _____

Class: _____   Period: _____

Directions: List the names of the students in your class. Place check marks when a student exhibits a behavior listed. The results can be used as part of a reward system established by the classroom teacher.

Classroom Behaviors

Student Name	On Time to Class	Prepared for Class: Pencil Paper Homework Textbook Notebook	Works Quietly in Class	Stays on Task	Participates in Class	Total Points

Form 4.2   Behavior Contract

Student name: _____   Date: _____

Teacher name: _____   Class: _____

Contract starts: _____

Contract ends: _____

Contract review dates: _____   _____   _____   _____   _____   _____

The student will

_____

_____

_____

_____

_____

_____

_____

The teacher will

_____

_____

_____

_____

_____

_____

_____

The student must fulfill his or her part of the contract to receive the agreed-upon reward from the teacher.

Student signature: _____

Teacher signature: _____

Parent/guardian signature: _____

Form 4.3   Student Progress Report

Student name: _____   Date: _____

Directions: Please check the column that accurately depicts the student's progress in the subject/behavior column and provide comments where necessary.

Subject/Behavior	Satisfactory	Needs Improvement
Reading		
English		
Math		
Science		
Social studies		
Written expression		
Follows class rules		
Exhibits appropriate behavior both inside and outside of class		
Respects personal and school property		
Participates in class		
Completes assigned work		
Follows directions		
Brings materials to class		

Student signature: _____

Teacher signature: _____

Parent signature: _____

Form 4.4   Classroom Policies and Procedures Checklist

Classroom Procedures Are Needed For

_____ How students are to enter the classroom

_____ How students are to exit the classroom

_____ How and when students will be excused to the restroom

_____ How and when students will get a drink of water

_____ Class schedule for academics or specialty classes

_____ How students are to respond or ask questions in the classroom

_____ How and when students will move around in the classroom

_____ Specifying appropriate student behavior when working with other students

_____ Where students are to place personal items: book bags, coats, lunch boxes, etc.

_____ How teacher will collect monies: lunch, field trip, book fines, etc.

_____ How students are to move in the hallway

_____ Other: _____

Classroom Policies Are Needed For

_____ Grading system or method

_____ Late work

_____ Class work

_____ Makeup work

_____ Homework

_____ Student tardiness

_____ Student attendance

_____ Reporting student progress

_____ Reporting student final grade

_____ Required class materials

_____ Assessment of students in the special and inclusive classroom

_____ Other: _____

Form 4.5 Classroom Management Plan Evaluation

School year: _____

Directions: I would appreciate your assistance with an important project that will help me make our classroom a better place to learn. PLEASE MAKE A LIST OF WHAT YOU LIKE BEST AND WHAT YOU WOULD LIKE TO CHANGE ABOUT OUR CLASSROOM. I have listed some areas you might want to consider at the bottom of the page. Thank you!

The things I like best about our classroom.	The things I would like to change in our classroom.

Areas to consider:

- Classroom color
- Classroom arrangement
- Seating arrangement
- Classroom rules and consequences
- Classroom policies and procedures (for example, how the teacher grades and how quickly the teacher returns completed work)
- Class activities
- Class games and materials
- Class field trips
- How the teacher communicates with me

Teaching All Students

5

When we work from the conviction that all children can learn, when we set high expectations, and we strengthen the curriculum, students rise to meet the challenges.

—Richard Riley

Teachers throughout the United States are confronting a multitude of challenges in their journeys to prepare students to meet the demands of a global economy. Although teachers continue to struggle with issues revolving around high drop-out rates, chronic absenteeism, and serious discipline problems of students, the No Child Left Behind Act (NCLB) is the challenge that is currently at the forefront for most educators. NCLB has placed an enormous amount of pressure on teachers to increase the academic achievement of all students, including students with disabilities. Special education teachers have been significantly affected by NCLB and thrust into the accountability arena with their general education colleagues. The movement throughout the nation of placing and educating more students with disabilities in general education classrooms or least restrictive environments is causing special education teachers to make necessary paradigm shifts. No longer can the special education teacher think in terms of "What instructional practices and strategies can I use to effectively meet the needs of my students with disabilities?" Instead, he or she must think in terms of "What instructional practices and strategies can I use to meet the needs of all students?" Both general and special education teachers must become data savvy and begin to routinely use qualitative and quantitative data for the purpose of instructional decision making and evaluating student progress. Teachers must arm themselves with the knowledge of how to interpret and use data to meet the accountability challenge.

The information contained in this chapter is designed to guide the beginning teacher through the planning and implementation of instruction for all students. The authors acknowledge that diversity exists among special education programs and delivery models; the authors contend, however, that the information provided in this chapter can be applied to most educational settings or programs, including the general education classroom. The authors provide the reader with the basics steps of instructional planning and implementation that will provide the framework for a successful teaching experience and list effective instructional strategies designed to reach all students. The authors have included all forms and resource information that will support the new teacher at the end of the chapter.

SECTION 1: PREPARING FOR INSTRUCTION

Step 1: Review the Individualized Education Program

The teacher must review each student's Individualized Education Program (IEP) and identify the academic goals and objectives that must be addressed during the school year. The IEP is the foundation and driving force behind all academic instruction for students with disabilities. The teacher should identify the following information before planning and implementing instructional plans:

- Specific skills to be taught
- Specific methods and materials to be used in the instruction process
- Specific methods of evaluating each objective
- Initiation and completion dates of goals and objectives
- Specific service provider/providers

The authors have developed an IEP Goals and Objectives Checklist form designed to assist the new special education teacher with instructional planning. After completing the checklist, the teacher should be able to map out his or her direction for academic instruction for the school year, collect or purchase appropriate instructional materials, and complete lesson plans that incorporate the instructional and evaluation methods recommended for each student.

Step 2: Selecting Instructional Materials

The special education teacher must begin the process of selecting instructional materials after reviewing each student's current IEP. The selection process can seem overwhelming and confusing for the new special education teacher; Mercer and Mercer (1993), however, suggest that teachers use the following plan when selecting instructional materials:

- Identify the curriculum areas in which materials are needed.
- Rank the areas from highest to lowest priority.
- List affordable materials that are designed to teach in the selected skill area or areas.
- Obtain the materials and evaluate them so that a decision can be made regarding a purchase. On request, many publishers will provide a sample of materials or a manual for the teacher to examine or field test. Also,

many school districts have resource or curriculum centers that contain materials for teachers to inspect. (p. 150)

The instructor should review and select instructional materials that are appropriate for students with disabilities and support the curriculum for the designated subject or skill areas. The authors strongly recommend that the new teacher use the instructional materials available in his or her school system when appropriate. In addition, the authors recommend that the new teacher consult with other special education teachers on staff for advice and guidance in the selection process. The authors have created the Classroom Teacher's Instructional Materials List to use during the selection process and provide the reader with a list of commercial publishers.

Step 3: Creating a Class Schedule

The new teacher must create a class schedule that is appropriate for his or her program or delivery model. Class schedules vary greatly among the various special education models and programs and between different grade levels. The special education teacher should design a class schedule that flows with the school's master schedule, is conducive to the schedules of inclusive students, and allows for teacher planning. Teachers in resource or self-contained settings should design a schedule that will accommodate academic instruction; students in inclusive classes; specialty, exploratory, or elective classes; lunch; and recess (when appropriate). An effective schedule is vital to the overall operation of the special education classroom. The class schedule provides class structure, ensures that instruction time for the core academic areas is maximized, and integrates lower priority classes with other miscellaneous activities. The following are suggestions for class schedules based on grade level:

Elementary Level (Mercer & Mercer, 1993, p. 128)

- Analyze the day's events.
- Plan opening exercises.
- Schedule academic instruction.
- Plan closing exercises.

Secondary Level

- Homeroom
- Academic instruction: school day divided into class periods (possibly six or seven classes a day, 50–55 minutes per class)
- Lunch
- Exploratory class (middle school)
- Elective class (high school)
- Transition program
- Planning
- Advisement

Materials or Resources

Form 5.1: IEP Goals and Objectives Checklist

Form 5.2: Classroom Teacher's Instructional Materials List

Resource 5.1: Guide to Locating Instructional Materials

Form 5.3: Class Schedule

SECTION 2: PLANNING AND IMPLEMENTING EFFECTIVE LESSON PLANS

The teacher should plan and implement lesson plans that take into consideration how each student receives and processes information, address the needs of the student, promote a sense of wonder and excitement within the student, and engage the student in the learning process. This section provides hints for better lesson planning and implementation; the authors suggest, however, that the teacher use the information listed here as a basic framework and then develop a system that fits his or her personal style. The authors have included a Weekly Lesson Plan form that the teacher may use when planning for instruction.

Instructional Planning Guide

- Plan lessons at least 1 week in advance.
- Set aside time each day to plan—do not try to do all your planning in 1 day.
- Collaborate and plan with the general education teacher in inclusive settings.
- Select objectives for each lesson to be taught.
- Write objectives on the board or post in highly visible location.
- Select supporting materials to reinforce lesson objectives or skills being taught.
- Make copies of all reinforcement materials in advance.
- Write all plans in a lesson plan book or in the format required by your school.
- Give a copy of your lesson plans to the designated person at your school.
- Secure all additional materials for the lesson in advance (e.g., videos, maps, and calculators).
- Prepare a weekly syllabus or homework calendar for students.
- Inform students in advance of all test dates.
- Make sure overhead or LCD projector and other equipment is in working order in advance of lesson presentation.
- Review all lessons prior to class period.

Implementation of Lesson Plans

- Preview Lesson
- Review previous lesson (make a link to prior knowledge).
- Introduce lesson or skill—create a sense of wonder in the student (motivate learner).

- Preteach lesson vocabulary.
- Pretest when appropriate.

Conduct Lesson

- Demonstrate skill: Explain and discuss with students.
- Provide opportunity for guided practice: Correct and discuss.
- Provide opportunity for independent practice: Correct and discuss.
- Provide opportunity for students to demonstrate skill (i.e., presentation and producing a product).
- Check on learning, and assess student progress.
- Reteach problem areas.

Conclude Lesson

- Require students to summarize lesson content ("what I know").
- Evaluate skill mastery.

Materials and Resources

Form 5.4: Weekly Lesson Plan

SECTION 3: INSTRUCTIONAL STRATEGIES FOR ALL STUDENTS

In this section, the authors provide the new teacher with instructional strategies that can be used with special and general education students. The strategies can be modified to fit the individual needs of students when appropriate. The authors provide a reference for each set of instructional strategies.

Strategy 1: Teacher-Directed Instruction (Southern Regional Education Board, 2001)

In a teacher-directed classroom, the teacher plans, shapes, and guides the learning process. Direct instruction is the best way to teach skills, procedures, and processes that are essential components of the curriculum (p. 6).

Strategy 2: Student-Centered Learning (Southern Regional Education Board, 2001)

Student-centered learning is based on the belief that active involvement by students increases learning and motivation. Good student-centered learning values the student's role in acquiring knowledge and understanding (p. 8).

a. *Cooperative learning:* Cooperative learning is an instructional strategy that encourages students to learn together but holds each student accountable for his or her learning (p. 8).

b. *Project-based learning:* A project-based approach to instruction presents students with problem-focused assignments that are meaningful, interesting, and valuable (p. 10).

c. *The Socratic method:* The Socratic method is a time-honored technique in which the teacher asks questions that lead students to examine the validity of a statement. The greatest challenge is to design thought-provoking questions that will engage students in productive discussions (p. 14).

d. *Independent research studies:* Independent research studies allow students to choose topics related to the subject of study. Students gather, record, evaluate, and organize information and draw conclusions based on what they have learned (p. 16).

e. *Reading and writing across the curriculum:* Reading and writing across the curriculum is an approach to learning in which teachers of all subjects use strategies that promote writing and reading comprehension (p. 17).

f. *Using technology in the classroom:* Integrating technology into instruction provides students with fresh ways to learn and opportunities to apply knowledge to new situations, thereby encouraging problem-solving and thinking skills (p. 32).

 1. Do not abandon successful lesson plans. Integrate technology into these plans when appropriate.

 2. Incorporate spreadsheets, databases, word processors, graphing calculators, presentation software, and other technology into the instructional programs of all content areas. Demonstrate how to use technology, and give students opportunities to use it.

 3. Use computer activities to reinforce instruction.

 4. Take "virtual field trips" to historical sites, art galleries, museums, or other interesting places worldwide. Make students responsible for designing the trips.

 5. Use computer simulations to explore real-world problems (p. 33).

Strategy 3: Graphic Organizers
(Thompson & Thompson, 2003, p. 2)

Graphic organizers are instructional tools that facilitate instruction and promote student learning (Figure 5.1):

a. Graphic organizers help students comprehend information through visual representation of concepts, ideas, and relationships. They provide the structure for short- and long-term memory.

b. Graphic organizers turn abstract concepts into concrete visual representations.

c. Understanding text structure is critical to reading comprehension. If students have a guide to the text structure, their comprehension is considerably higher than when they rely only on reading and memorization.

d. The most important question a teacher can answer is: "How do I want students to think about my content?" Then, the teacher selects a graphic organizer that facilitates that type of thinking.

Figure 5.1   Graphic Organizer Sample: Compare and Contrast

e. The use of graphic organizers produces learning effects that are substantial and long-lasting.

SOURCE: Used with permission of Dr. Max Thompson, Learning Concepts, Boone, NC.

Strategy 4: Summarizing Strategies (Thompson & Thompson, 2003)

According to Drs. Max Thompson and Julia Thomason, the authors of *Learning-Focused Strategies Notebook*, having students summarize what they are learning is important to the learning process for the following reasons:

a. Summarizing is perhaps the key thinking skill for learning.
b. Summarizing is a learning strategy, not a teaching strategy. Learners must summarize themselves for the learning to construct meaning.
c. When summarizing, students create a "schema" for the information and remember it better and longer.
d. Teachers find out what students have internalized, understood, and remembered.
e. When students summarize, their confusions, misconceptions, or misunderstandings surface, and teachers can then adapt future teaching accordingly. It is key to knowing when and on what to reteach.
f. Student summarizing should be distributed throughout a lesson, not just at the end (p. 2).

Summarizing Strategy 1: Ticket Out the Door! (Thompson & Thompson, 2003, p. 3)

The ticket out the door strategy allows teachers to assess to what extent students have learned during the lesson. The following is a sample prompt:

- One's tell two's three major points from today's lesson. Two's write it down. (Or call on two's.)
- Make sure you have answered the lesson's essential question.
- If either of you are unsure about something from the lesson, please note topic or questions you have.
- Put your "ticket" in the basket as you leave.
    Or
- Share your "ticket" with the whole class.
    Or
- Share your "ticket" with another pair.

Summarizing Strategy 2: 3-2-1
(Thompson & Thompson, 2003, p. 4)

- 3-2-1 is a summarizing strategy used to help students think about what they have learned in the lesson, reading, video, presentation, and so on. The students write approximately three things . . . then two things . . . and then one more thing. What they write about is up to the teacher based on the lesson. This strategy can also be modified to only have 2-1 (two item headings instead of three). At the end of a lesson, video, reading, or presentation, write on the board the 3-2-1 outline.
- Ask students to write on the three headings, making sure they understand that for (3) they must write three ideas, for (2) they must write two ideas, and for (1) they must write one idea.
- Use their writing as a ticket out the door or as a homework assignment.
- Have students share their answers in pairs, groups, or with the class.

Example: Federal government system:

> Write: three ways the system has checks and balances;
> two ways that the system effects you; and
> one thing you think could make the system better.

Materials or Resources

Resource 5.2: Technology-Connected Lesson Plan Form

SECTION 4: EVALUATING STUDENT PROGRESS

The evaluation of student progress and mastery of academic skills is an essential step in the instructional process. The beginning teacher will quickly discover that the best way to obtain a total picture of a student's level of mastery is to use a variety of informal assessments. The authors have found performance-based assessments to be extremely useful in assessing student learning. Performance-based assessments require students to demonstrate their knowledge of acquired skills. The newsletter titled *Improving America's Schools: A Newsletter on Issues in School Reform* (U.S. Department of Education, 1996) notes that performance assessments may include any of the following:

- Open-ended or constructed response items: items asking students to respond in their own words—to "construct" their answers—to questions that may have multiple correct answers. Students usually reason out their solutions as part of their answers. Usually, students can answer these questions in a few minutes, and in this way these assessments differ from some of the performance activities described next (p. 1).

- Performance-based items or events: questions, tasks, or activities that require students to perform an action. Although performances can involve demonstrations or presentations, typically they involve students explaining how they would answer the question or solve a problem by writing a few sentences or paragraphs, drawing and explaining a diagram, or performing an experiment. Such tasks may take from 15 minutes to 1 hour or more and may involve some work with a group of students who think through the answers and later provide their own individually written answers (p. 1).

- Projects or experiments: extended performance tasks that may take several days or even several weeks to complete. Students generate problems, consider options, propose solutions, and demonstrate their solutions. Students often work in groups, at least during some of the project, to analyze options and consider ways to present their thinking and conclusions (p. 1).

- Portfolios: collections of student work that show teachers and others who may "score" portfolios the range and quality of student work over a period of time and in various content areas. There are almost as many approaches to compiling and evaluating portfolios as there are proponents of this form of assessment. Portfolios can be used both formally and informally; ideally, portfolios capture the evolution of students' ideas and can be used instructionally and as progress markers for students, teachers, and program evaluators (p. 2).

Materials and Resources

Resource 5.3: Computer Software to Assist Teachers in Managing Student Data

Form 5.1   IEP Goals and Objectives Checklist

Student name: _____   School year: _____

Directions: Complete the information below upon review of each student's current IEP.

Skill Area	Recommended Instructional Methods	Required Instructional Materials	Recommended Method of Evaluation

Skill areas: Academic, social, daily living, leisure, transition, or other.

Instructional method: Modeling, guided practice, reinforcements, drill and practice, use of manipulatives, chaining, whole language approach, direct instruction, learning strategies, multisensory approach, or other.

Instructional materials: Textbooks, supporting materials, manipulatives, concrete materials, or other.

Methods of evaluation: Observation, work samples, unit tests, surveys, interviews, criterion-reference tests, student portfolios, or other.

Form 5.2 Classroom Teacher's Instructional Materials List

Teacher name: _____ Date: _____

Program: _____ Room: _____

Skill Area	Instructional Materials (List and Describe)	Quantity Requested	Company Name, Address, Telephone Number, and Fax Number

Resource 5.1   Guide to Locating Instructional Materials

A. D. D. Warehouse
300 NW 70th Avenue, Suite 102
Plantation, FL 33337
Telephone: 800-233-9273
Fax: 954-792-8545
Web site: www.addawarehouse.com

Academic Communication Associates, Inc.
Publication Center, Department 62E
4149 Avenida de la Plata
P.O. Box 4279
Oceanside, CA 92052-4279
Telephone: 760-758-9593
Fax: 760-758-1604

Academic Therapy Publications
20 Commercial Boulevard
Novato, CA 94949-6191
Telephone: 415-883-3314
Fax: 415-883-3720
Web site: www.atpub.com

Addison Wesley Longman Publishing Company
1 Jacob Way
Reading, MA 01867
Telephone: 800-552-2499
Fax: 800-284-8292
Web site: www.awl.com

American Guidance Service (AGS)
4201 Woodland Road
Circle Pines, MN 55014-1796
Telephone: 800-328-2560
Fax: 612-786-9077
Web site: www.agsnet.com

Bureau for At-Risk Youth
135 Dupont Street
P.O. Box 760
Plainview, NY 11803-0760
Telephone: 800-999-6884
Fax: 516-349-5521
Web site: www.at-risk.com

C. H. Stoelting Company
620 Wheat Lane
Wood Dale, IL 60191
Telephone: 630-860-9700
Fax: 630-860-9775
Web site: www.stoeltingco.com/tests

Cambridge Development Laboratory, Inc.
86 West Street
Waltham, MA 02451
Telephone: 800-637-0047
Fax: 781-890-2894
Web site: www.cdlspecial.com

Capstone Curriculum Publishing
151 Good Counsel Drive
P.O. Box 669
Mankato, MN 56002-0669
Telephone: 888-574-6711
Fax: 888-574-6183

Center on Education and Work
University of Wisconsin–Madison
School of Education
964 Educational Sciences Building
1025 W. Johnson Street
Madison, WI 53706-1796
Telephone: 800-446-0399
Fax: 608-262-9197
Web site: www.cew.wise.edu

Channing L. Bete Company, Inc.
200 State Road
South Deerfield, MA 01373-0200
Telephone: 877-896-8532
Fax: 800-499-6464
Web site: www.channing-bete.com

Child's Work Child's PLAY
Genesis Direct, Inc.
100 Plaza Drive
Secaucus, NJ 07094-3613
Telephone: 800-962-1141
Fax: 201-583-3644
Web site: www.childsplay.com

Curriculum Associates
5 Esquire Road, N
Billerica, MA 01862-2589
Telephone: 800-225-0248
Fax: 800-366-1158
Web site: www.curriculumassociates.com

EBSCO Curriculum Materials
Box 11521
Birmingham, AL 35202-1521
Telephone: 800-633-8623

Fax: 205-991-1482
Web site: www.ecmtest.com

Educational Design
345 Hudson Street
New York, NY 10014-4502
Telephone: 800-221-9372
Fax: 212-675-6922
Web site: www.educationaldesign.com

Educators Publishing Service, Inc.
31 Smith Place
Cambridge, MA 02138
Telephone: 800-225-5750
Fax: 617-547-0412
Web site: www.epsbooks.com

Funtastic Therapy
RD 4 Box 14, John White Road
Cranberry, NJ 08512
Telephone: 800-531-3176
Fax: 609-275-0488

Glencoe/McGraw-Hill
P.O. Box 508
Columbus, OH 43216
Telephone: 800-334-7344
Fax: 614-860-1877
Web site: www.glencoe.com

Globe Fearon Publishers
4350 Equity Drive
P.O. Box 2649
Columbus, OH 43216
Telephone: 800-848-9500
Fax: 614-771-7361

Greenwood Publishing Group, Inc.
88 Post Road West
Westport, CT 06881
Telephone: 203-226-3571
Fax: 203-222-1502
Web site: www.greenwood.com

Hawthorne Educational Services
800 Gray Oak Drive
Columbia, MO 65201
Telephone: 800-542-1673
Fax: 800-442-9509

Huby's Ltd.
School To Work Catalog
Department W99
P.O. Box 9117
Jackson, WY 83002
Telephone: 800-543-0998
Fax: 800-518-2514

J. Weston Walch Publishers
321 Valley Street
P.O. Box 658
Portland, ME 04104-0658
Telephone: 800-341-6094
Fax: 207-772-3105

Kaplan Concepts for Exceptional Children
P.O. Box 609
1310 Lewisville-Clemmons Road
Lewisville, NC 27023-0609
Telephone: 800-334-2014
Fax: 800-452-7526
Web site: www.kaplanco.com

Lakeshore Learning Materials
2695 East Dominquez Street
P.O. Box 6261
Carson, CA 90749
Telephone: 800-421-5354
Fax: 310-537-5403
Web site: www.lakeshorelearning.com

PCI Educational Publishing
2800 NE Loop 410, Suite 105
San Antonio, TX 78218-1525
Telephone: 800-594-4263
Fax: 888-259-8284
Web site: www.pcicatalog.com

Prufrock Press
P.O. Box 8813
Waco, TX 76714-8813
Telephone: 800-998-2208
Fax: 800-240-0333
Web site: www.prufrock.com/

Remedia Publications
10135 East Via Linda, Suite D124
Scottsdale, AZ 85258-5312
Telephone: 800-826-4740

(Continued)

Resource 5.1 (Continued)

Fax: 602-661-9901
Web site: www.rempub.com

Research Press
P.O. Box 9177
Champaign, IL 61826
Telephone: 800-510-2707
Fax: 217-252-1221
Web site: www.researchpress.com

Resources for Educators
P.O. Box 362916
Des Moines, IA 50336-2916
Telephone: 800-491-0551
Fax: 800-835-5327
Web site: www.phdirect.com

Saddleback Educational, Inc.
3503 Cadillac Avenue, Building F-9
Costa Mesa, CA 92618-2767
Telephone: 949-860-2500
Fax: 949-860-2508

Scholastic, Inc.
P.O. Box 7502
Jefferson City, MO 65102
Telephone: 800-724-6527
Fax: 573-635-7630

Scott Foresman/Addison-Wesley
School Services
1 Jacob Way
Reading, MA 01867
Telephone: 800-552-2259
Fax: 800-333-3328
Web site: www.sf.aw.com

Slosson
P.O. Box 280

East Aurora, NY 14052-0280
Telephone: 888-756-7766
Fax: 800-655-3840
Web site: www.slosson.com

SRA/McGraw-Hill
220 East Danieldale Road
DeSoto, TX 75115-2490
Telephone: 800-843-8855
Fax: 214-228-1982
Web site: www.sra-4kids.com

Teacher Ideas Press
P.O. Box 6633
Englewood, CO 80155-6633
Telephone: 800-237-6124
Fax: 303-220-8843
Web site: www.lu.com

Things for Learning
P.O. Box 908
Rutherfordton, NC 28139
Telephone: 800-228-6178
Fax: 704-287-9506

Western Psychological
Services
12031 Wilshire Boulevard
Los Angeles, CA 90025
Telephone: 800-648-8857
Fax: 310-478-7838

Wieser Educational, Inc.
30085 Comercio
Rancho Santa Margarita,
CA 92688-2106
Telephone: 800-880-4433
Fax: 800-949-0209

Form 5.3   Class Schedule

Teacher: _____   School year: _____

Semester: _____

Time	Subject/Activity
–	
–	
–	
–	
–	
–	
–	
–	
–	

Form 5.4   Weekly Lesson Plan

Class or subject: _____   Week of: _____

Class time: _____   Period: _____

Textbook: _____

Class roster: _____

_____

_____

Chapter/topic: _____

Lesson objectives: _____

_____

_____

_____

Day	Activities/Content	Homework
Monday Date:		
Tuesday Date:		
Wednesday Date:		
Thursday Date:		
Friday Date:		

Notes:

_____

_____

_____

Resource 5.2   Technology-Connected Lesson Plan Form

Lesson title: _____

Subject area: _____

Topic: _____

Performance Objectives

After completion of the lesson, students will be able to (use action verbs):

1. _____

2. _____

3. _____

4. _____

5. _____

Lesson Format or Procedure

_____

_____

_____

_____

_____

_____

Assessment of Student Learning

Explain in detail how students will be assessed upon completion of lesson:

_____

_____

_____

_____

_____

_____

(Continued)

Resource 5.6 (Continued)

Classroom Management Strategies

_____

_____

_____

_____

_____

_____

Required Materials or Equipment

_____

_____

_____

_____

_____

_____

_____

_____

Related URLs: _____

_____

_____

_____

_____

SOURCE: Adapted from the Georgia Department of Education–Georgia Educational Technology Training Centers _Integrating TECHnology_ Lesson Plan Format.

Resource 5.3   Computer Software to Assist Teachers in Managing Student Data

Note: The computer software programs listed here are only a sampling of grading programs that are available to assist teachers with managing student data. The authors recommend that the beginning teacher check with his or her school's technology support personnel regarding similar programs available at the school.

Class Action Gradebook
www.ClassActionGradebook.com

1st Class Gradebook
www.1st-class-software.com

Grade Genie!
www.kilowattsoftware.com/GradeGeniePage.htm

Gradebook Power
www.wiscocomputing.com/gradebook.htm

GradeBook—Teacher's Electronic Grade Book Grading Software
www.rredware.com

GradeQuick
www.teacherease.com

Making the Grade Teacher Grade Book Software
www.cri-mms.com/Making_the_Grade.html

Online Grading Software
www.gradenetwork.com

Teacher's Toolbox Deluxe
www.5dollarsoftware.com/tetode.html

VAR Grade
www.varedsw.com/products.htm

Preparing for a Successful Parent-Teacher Conference

The more the school and the family are joined as partners in educating young people, the greater the child's chances for success.

—Harry Wong and Rosemary Wong

A parent conference is an excellent two-way communication strategy to use to build rapport and trust with parents. Parent-teacher conferences tend to be more personal and productive, and they provide less chance for the misinterpretation of information. Special education teachers typically conduct numerous parent conferences during the school year and organize and facilitate many more involving teachers, administrators, and other support personnel. Minke and Anderson (2003) found two primary themes to be supported in traditional parent conferences: "Parents and teachers agreed that conferences are important opportunities for information exchange, with the major purpose of teachers giving information to parents; and parents and teachers approach conferences with varying degrees of trepidation" (p. 57).

The new special education teacher can perfect his or her communication skills that are essential for a successful parent-teacher conference by focusing on developing positive speaking, rephrasing, and attentive listening skills. Berger (1995) provides teachers with the following qualities of good communicators:

1. Give their total attention to the speaker.

2. Restate the parents' concerns.

3. Show respect for the other person.

4. Recognize the parents' feelings.

5. Tailor discussions to fit the parents' ability to handle the situation.

6. Do not touch off the fuse of a parent who might not be able to handle a child's difficulties.

7. Emphasize that concerns are no one's fault.

8. Remember that no one ever wins an argument.

9. Protect the parents' egos.

10. Focus on one issue at a time.

11. Listen.

12. Become allies with parents. (p. 276)

Parents need to leave each conference with the feeling that someone truly understands their concerns and confident that any plans or strategies developed during the conference will be implemented and monitored by school officials. Most often, if the new teacher uses good conferencing skills, rapport will be established, and the foundation will be laid for a good parent-teacher relationship. Unfortunately, conferences are not always pleasant experiences for school officials or parents, and sometimes a satisfactory resolution to an identified problem or concern is elusive to all in attendance. The beginning teacher must be prepared to deal with the dissatisfaction or anger of parents. The authors found a list of suggestions created by Dr. Michael A. Morehead to be beneficial for teachers and other school personnel (Resource 6.1).

The objectives of a parent-teacher conference depend on the purpose of the meeting. The following are conference categories most frequently used by the special education teacher: progress report, problem solving, and the mandated Individualized Education Program (IEP). The parent-teacher conference requires a tremendous amount of preplanning by the special education teacher. The authors provide the reader with a recommended list of essential tasks that generally contribute to the success of most conferences and separate lists for the progress report and problem-solving conferences that will assist the teacher in his or her preparation and ensure a successful and productive parent-teacher meeting. All information pertaining to IEP conferences is provided in Chapter 8.

The new teacher must remember that the parents are the true "experts" with regard to the student and often have beneficial information pertaining to strategies that have historically "worked" or "not worked" with the student. Parents should be viewed as consultants and valuable members of the student's educational team. The teacher should provide the parents with all information or documents pertaining to the meeting prior to the conference date. Parents must prepare for conferences in the same manner as the teacher to maximize the benefits of a school conference. Resource 6.2 provides information for parents in need of assistance in conference preparation. Finally, the authors remind the first-year teacher that "communication, both nonverbal and verbal, is the 'stuff' that initiates, builds, maintains, and destroys relationships" (Miller, Wackman, Nunnally, & Miller, 1988, p. 9).

ESSENTIAL TASKS FOR ALL PARENT-TEACHER CONFERENCES

Preconference Tasks

_____ Prior written notification of meeting should be given to the parents or guardians and other conference participants (at least 7 to 10 working days in advance).

_____ Conference notification should include the following (see Form 6.1):

a. Date, time, and exact location of conference
b. Purpose of conference
c. List of people and their respective positions to attend conference (Include student's name on the notification. It is mandatory that a student of any age who has a disability be invited if the purpose of the meeting is to consider or discuss transition services.)
d. Request confirmation of attendance from all invitees. List special education teacher's name and telephone number as contact person for all conference inquiries.

_____ Select and reserve conference location. This location must be a neutral area that is comfortable and free from interruptions, such as the school's main conference room or media center's conference room.

_____ Formulate a meeting agenda and distribute to parents or guardians and all school personnel invited to conference well in advance of the designated meeting date (letter or e-mail).

_____ Send parents or guardians a conference preparation handout (Resource 6.2) prior to meeting.

_____ Telephone or e-mail parents or guardians 2 days prior to conference as a friendly reminder.

_____ Confirm conference with school personnel 2 days prior to conference through e-mail or letter (Form 6.2).

_____ Ensure the following school personnel have been invited to the following conferences:

a. Progress report conference: parents or guardians, general education teachers of included students, school counselor, special education teacher, and additional special education staff
b. Problem-solving conference: parents or guardians, school administrator, general education teachers of included students, school counselor, special education coordinator or support person, and special education teacher or special education staff or both

c. IEP conference: parents or guardians, at least one general education teacher of included students, at least one special education teacher, school or special education administrator, related services, transition service participants, and the student (if appropriate).

Conference Tasks

_____ Introduce school principal, faculty, and special education personnel to parents or guardians.

_____ Give parent rights booklet to the parents or guardians when appropriate.

_____ State the purpose of the conference.

_____ The special education teacher should appoint an individual to take copious notes during the meeting and highlight all significant information in the minutes of the meeting.

_____ The special education teacher should close the conference by summarizing all information discussed and review any additions to the student's IEP.

_____ All information discussed and plans developed during the meeting should be written on minutes form and signed by all people attending the conference (see Form 6.3).

_____ Give parents or guardians a copy of the conference minutes.

Postconference Tasks

_____ Send parents or guardians a summary of the meeting in a letter format and include the following (see Form 6.4):

a. Thank parents for attending the meeting.
b. Send any documents requested by the parents during the meeting.
c. Indicate the best school hours and days to reach the special education teacher if parents have further questions.
d. Conclude the letter with a positive comment about the student.

ESSENTIAL INFORMATION FOR THE PROGRESS REPORT CONFERENCE

Directions: The following information must be collected and reviewed by the special education teacher prior to the progress report conference. All collected documentation should be shared with the parents in advance of the scheduled meeting.

Student Information

_____ Current student school attendance record:

    a. Request a copy of the student's attendance record from your school's attendance office.

    b. Review the student's tardy record.

    c. Request that all teachers of included students note attendance and tardy information on the student's monitor form (see Chapter 3).

_____ Current student school discipline record:

    a. Request a summary report of the student's discipline record from the school's discipline office or the student's discipline administrator.

    b. Review the student's discipline record for the following:
        1. Description of discipline referrals or classroom infractions or both
        2. Discipline referrals date and time
        3. Name of referring school official

_____ Review student's academic school record with the school counselor:

    a. Review previous academic achievements.

    b. Review student's academic portfolio.

    c. Review the total number of earned high school units or credits.

    d. Review the program of study or academic emphasis the student has decided to pursue.

Classroom Information

_____ Review the following information from general education teachers for students in inclusive settings:

   ___ Class participation   ___ Class/daily work   ___ Portfolio

   ___ Test grades   ___ On-task behavior   ___ Overall performance

   ___Quiz grades   ___ Tardy/absent

_____ Review information from special education teacher:

   _____ Current mastery of IEP objectives

   _____ Current successful instructional strategies

   _____ Current successful behavior modification strategies

   _____ Status on previously developed plans or strategies

   _____ Overall performance in the special education classroom

ESSENTIAL INFORMATION FOR THE PROBLEM-SOLVING CONFERENCE

Directions: The following information must be collected and reviewed by the special education teacher prior to the problem-solving conference. All collected documentation should be shared with the parents in advance of the scheduled meeting.

A. Identify Presenting Behavior Problem

Problem involves

1. Student self-control

2. Student affect: enthusiasm, leadership, followership, responsibility, reactions to rewards and contingencies.

3. Social conventions: manners, courtesy, and respect for others and their property

Problem occurs

1. Special education classroom

2. General education classroom

3. Recess

4. Field trips

5. School bus

6. Bathroom

7. Hallway

8. Lunchroom

B. Identify Presenting Academic Problem

Problem involves

1. Student's performance in the areas of reading, spelling, English, science, social studies, math, or other

2. Student's performance on tests

3. Student's performance on quizzes

4. Student's homework completion

5. Student's completion of assigned projects

Problem occurs

1. General education classroom or setting

   Class: _____ Teacher: _____

2. Special education classroom or setting

   Class: _____ Teacher: _____

Resource 6.1   Dealing With the Anger of Parents

1. Have someone else present (teacher, administor, etc.).

2. Offer them a seat in a private setting—get off your feet.

3. Wait and listen.

4. Do not become defensive—be aware of tone of voice.

5. Speak softly and slowly, remain calm, and be aware of your posture.

6. Show genuine interest in the student—express this.

7. Do not fear anger—understand its origins.

8. Try to determine the cause of the anger.

9. Sometimes suggest a later meeting time.

10. Use phrases that are placating.

11. Not all parents are going to leave feeling good.

12. Acknowledge their anger—convey concern.

13. Avoid using angry responses, sarcasm, or negative nonverbal cues.

14. Seek assistance or support from principal or counselor.

Placating Responses

a. "I feel uncomfortable discussing this now. Could we set up a time we could meet that would be convenient?"

b. "I can appreciate how frustrating . . ."

c. "We are here to help your child and have only his best interest at heart."

d. "Let me see if I understand what you are concerned about."

e. "What do you want me to do? How do you want me to accomplish this?" Follow with "What can we do together?"

SOURCE: Used with permission from Michael A. Morehead, Associate Dean, College of Education, New Mexico State University.

Resource 6.2   Parent Tips for Conference Preparation

Before the Conference

- Make arrangements for your other children, if necessary. The conference is for you and your child's teacher; small children can be distracting and take time away from the discussion (Shea & Bauer, 1991, p. 146).

- Make a list of your questions or areas of concern that need to be addressed during the conference.

- Bring any documentation that you feel will assist school staff to better understand your child.

- Be prepared to take notes.

During the Conference

- Take notes.

- Convey your concerns or direct your questions to appropriate school staff.

- Listen to all responses.

- Ask for clarification on information that you do not understand.

- Discuss suggestions or strategies that the classroom teacher can implement in the classroom that will address the identified academic or behavior problem.

- Ask for suggestions or strategies that you can implement at home that will address the identified academic or behavior problem.

- Make plans to meet at a future date to evaluate the effectiveness of all strategies.

- Ask the meeting chairperson to summarize all information discussed at the conclusion of the meeting.

After the Conference

- Request a copy of the meeting minutes.

- Review your notes.

- Contact the chair of the meeting if you need clarification or continue to have areas of concern.

- Maintain a file of all meeting minutes and your personal notes.

Form 6.1   Conference Notification

Date: _____

Student name: _____   Grade: _____

Conference date and time: _____

Location: _____

Conference participants (name and position):

_____   _____

_____   _____

_____   _____

_____   _____

Conference purpose:

_____

_____

_____

_____

Requested information:

_____ Attendance   _____ Test grades

_____ Tardy   _____ Quiz grades

_____ Discipline   _____ On-task behavior

_____ Other:_____

_____

_____

_____

_____

Form 6.2   Conference Reminder

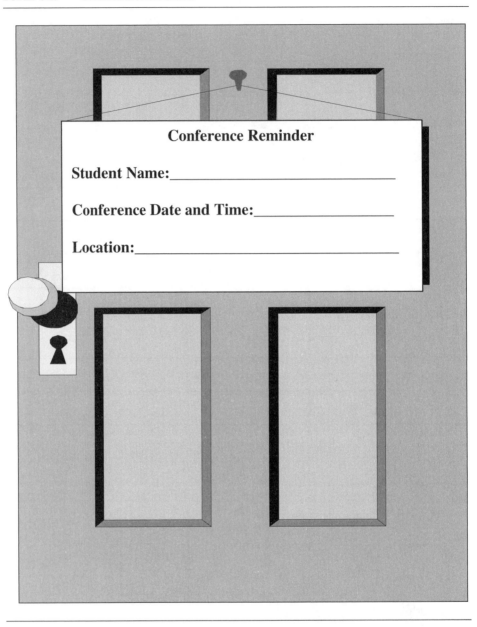

Conference Reminder

Student Name:_____

Conference Date and Time:_____

Location:_____

Form 6.3   Conference Minutes

Date: _____

Student name: _____   Grade: _____

Current placement: _____

Conference purpose:

_____

_____

_____

Conference summary:

_____

_____

_____

_____

_____

_____

_____

_____

Conference participants:

_____   _____

_____   _____

_____   _____

_____   _____

Form 6.4   Conference Summary

Date: _____

Dear _____

_____

_____

_____

_____

_____

_____

_____

_____

_____

_____

_____

_____

_____

Sincerely,

Enclosures

_____ Meeting minutes   _____ IEP documents

_____ Behavior contracts   _____ Academic strategies

_____ Behavior strategies   _____ Other

Understanding Educational Assessments

The desire to know is far more important than achievement and/or performance measures.

— G. Caine and R. Caine

Carr and Harris (2001) define assessment as

the process of quantifying, describing, gathering data about, or giving feedback about performance. Assessment results are used to identify instructional practices that should be improved, to focus professional development for teachers, and to supply new or different instructional resources for learners. (p. 175)

The beginning special education teacher will be exposed to a variety of educational assessments during the course of his or her career and should become familiar with the most common assessments that are administered not only to students with disabilities but also to all students due to the new requirements of No Child Left Behind (NCLB). Traditionally, the expectation was that these new professionals would have a basic knowledge of the educational assessments used to screen, diagnose, place, and plan programs for students with disabilities; the No Child Left Behind Act of 2001, however, has placed a new emphasis on using educational assessments as an accountability measure. One of the four guiding principles of NCLB is the stronger accountability for results. According to the information provided by the U.S. Department of Education, this principle involves the creation of standards in each state for what a child should know and learn in reading and math in Grades 3 through 8. With those standards in place, student progress and achievement will be measured according to state tests designed to match those state standards and given to every child every year. The expectation under NCLB is that students with disabilities will achieve at the same level as nondisabled students. Thurlow, Elliott, and Ysseldyke (1998) state,

> The reauthorization of the Individuals with Disabilities Education Act (IDEA), which funds special education programs, also requires that states report on the participation of students with disabilities in their state assessment programs and that an alternate assessment be used for those students who cannot be included in the statewide assessment program. (p. 7)

In light of this information, the number of students with disabilities taking high-stakes tests is on the rise throughout the country, and the special education teacher along with the Individualized Education Program (IEP) team are ultimately responsible for designing appropriate accommodations that will enable students to participate in the assessment process. To develop appropriate accommodations, the new teacher must possess a working knowledge of the assessments most commonly used in his or her school system and the acceptable or allowable modifications for those assessments. The new teacher must also be proficient in the administration of educational assessments and the interpretation of students' test results for the purpose of measuring student progress, program planning, instructional decision making, and accurately conveying all information to parents.

In this chapter, the authors discuss four strategies that are designed to reacquaint the beginning teacher with basic test and measurement information, to increase his or her overall knowledge of the levels of educational assessments, to assist the new teacher in obtaining a clear understanding of the IDEA '97 rules and regulations governing assessments for students with disabilities, and to provide a brief overview of assessment accommodations. The authors encourage the teacher to review his or her district's policies and procedures pertaining to student assessments before administering any tests and releasing student results. After reviewing the information in this chapter, the new teacher should be able to administer and interpret educational assessments with precision and confidence.

SECTION 1: REVIEW BASIC TEST AND MEASUREMENT INFORMATION

- Standardized tests

These tests are commercially prepared by experts in measurement and subject matter. They provide methods for obtaining samples of behavior under uniform procedures, and scoring is usually objective. Typically, a standardized test has been administered to a norm group (or groups) so that a person's performance can be interpreted by comparing it to the performance of others—that is, the test is norm-referenced (Mehrens & Lehmann, 1987, pp. 7–8).

- Test classification

  A. Cognitive measures: These are measures of maximum performance (how well a person will do when motivated to obtain as high a score as possible).
     1. Aptitude tests: These tests are designed to predict success in some future learning activity.
     2. Achievement tests: These tests are designed to indicate the degree of success in some past learning activity.

  B. Noncognitive measures: These are measures of typical behavior (procedures of this type are concerned with what the individual will do rather than what he or she can do).
     1. Interest inventories
     2. Personality inventories
     3. Attitude inventories

- Test characteristics

The following is a list of components that are essential when determining the adequacy of any assessment (formal or informal):

  A. Reliability: This refers to the consistency and stability of assessment results.
  B. Validity: This refers to the meaningfulness and appropriateness of the uses and interpretations to be made of assessment results. Validity is the most significant aspect of any test.
  C. Normative information: A comparison can be made of one student's results to those of other students who have taken the same test. According to Linn and Gronlund (1995), there are four basic types of test norms:
     1. Grade norms (grade equivalents): Grade group in which student's raw score is average. Note: Grade equivalents should never be interpreted literally; at best, they are only a rough guide as to the level of test performance.
     2. Percentile norms (percentile ranks or percentile scores): Percentage of students in the reference group who fall below student's raw score.
     3. Standard-score norms (standard scores): Distance of student's raw score above or below the mean of the reference group in terms of standard deviation units (p. 444).
     4. Stanines: Stanines are essentially groups of percentile ranks, with the entire group of scores divided into nine parts, with the largest number of individuals falling in the middle stanines and fewer students falling at the extremes. Few tests in common usage use stanines today, although these scores can be useful in understanding the relative range of a student's performance (Canter, 1998, p. 119).

Note: The teacher should always check the latest copyright date to ensure that the norms have been updated in an effort to keep the test current.

- Test interpretation

    A. Norm-referenced interpretation: This describes the performance in terms of the relative position held in some known group. Individual scores are compared with standard or group scores. A norm-referenced test is designed to provide a measure of performance that is interpretable in terms of an individual's relative standing in some known group.

Example: Jane typed better than 85% of the class members.

    B. Criterion-referenced interpretation: This describes the specific performance that was demonstrated. The criterion-referenced test is designed to provide a measure of performance that is interpretable in terms of a clearly defined and delimited domain of learning task.

Example: Jane typed 40 words per minute without error.

SECTION 2: UNDERSTAND THE LEVELS OF EDUCATIONAL ASSESSMENTS IN SCHOOLS

Educational assessments serve as tools to collect information pertaining to a student's performance in the school setting. Students with disabilities typically undergo a variety of educational assessments at various levels prior to being placed in a designated special education program or setting. The first level of assessment usually begins in the general education classroom, where the teacher identifies a student who consistently fails to perform academically or exhibits frequent inappropriate behavior. The special education teacher can be asked to review the student's work samples or complete a classroom observation. The new special education teacher should be able to determine if there is a substantial amount of evidence to refer the student for diagnostic testing. Diagnostic testing is usually the second level of educational assessment. The school counselor or special education teacher can be responsible for specific diagnostic testing at the school level. The student should be referred to the third assessment level if the diagnostic assessments continue to identify deficit or problem areas. At the third level, a licensed school psychologist usually conducts a comprehensive educational assessment. A battery of tests is administered to the student to measure the student's intellectual aptitudes, academic achievement, acuity, and learning style. In addition, classroom observations are conducted to document how the student functions academically, behaviorally, and socially in the classroom. Student work samples are collected from the classroom teacher. An adaptive behavior scale is usually completed if the student is suspected of being intellectually disabled. For initial referrals, the parents complete an in-depth developmental and medical history, and the student's permanent school record is reviewed. The school psychologist compiles all test results (formal and informal), observations, work samples, and parent and school history information and completes the final assessment report. The report is presented to a team of educators, the student's parents, and the student (when appropriate), and the results are explained and discussed in-depth. This report is the basis for student placement and the development of an IEP.

SECTION 3: KNOW THE CURRENT IDEA RULES AND REGULATIONS PERTAINING TO ASSESSING STUDENTS WITH DISABILITIES

The special education teacher must know and understand the rules and regulations that pertain to the assessment of students with disabilities. The following information is located in the Individuals with Disabilities Education Act of 1975, Section 300.347:

> (5)(i) A statement of any individual modifications in the administration of State or districtwide assessments of student achievement that are needed in order for the child to participate in the assessment; and
>
> (ii) If the IEP team determines that the child will not participate in a particular State or districtwide assessment of student achievement (or part of an assessment), a statement of (a) why the assessment is not appropriate for the child; and (b) how the child will be assessed.

According to the IDEA amendments of 2000, students who are unable to participate in state or districtwide testing must be given an alternate assessment. Browder et al. (2004) state, "Although not limited to this population, most students with severe disabilities (severe cognitive disabilities, multiple disabilities, severe autism, deaf-blindness) require an alternate assessment" (p. 211). Alternate assessments are instruments designed to obtain information pertaining to student performance. Alternate assessments can be almost anything. States are required to have alternate assessments, and the beginning teacher must obtain all information pertaining to his or her state's assessment. The authors have provided a Web site list that will assist with acquiring this information.

SECTION 4: REVIEW OF APPROPRIATE ASSESSMENT ACCOMMODATIONS

The special education teacher in conjunction with the IEP team is responsible for determining if a student with a disability will participate in state or districtwide testing. In most states, the IEP team also determines the need for a student to receive accommodations when taking an educational assessment. Thurlow et al. (1998) define accommodations as "changes in testing materials or procedures that enable the student with disabilities to participate in an assessment in a way that allows abilities to be assessed rather than disabilities" (pp. 27–28). In addition, Thurlow et al. identified the following types of accommodations:

- Setting accommodations
- Timing accommodations
- Scheduling accommodations
- Presentation accommodations
- Response accommodations
- Other accommodations (out-of-level testing, motivational accommodations, and test preparation)

All selected accommodations must parallel those provided to the student with disabilities in the general or special education classroom.

Materials or Resources

Form 7.1: Test Administration Checklist

Resource 7.1: Educational Assessments

Resource 7.2: Possible Modifications for Students With Disabilities

Form 7.1   Test Administration Checklist

The following checklist will guide the new special education teacher through his or her first test administration. The checklist is divided into three main sections. Space is provided for the teacher to add additional items to each section.

Prior to Test

_____ Send parent notification of test date and time. Request parent permission as directed by school system policy.

_____ Inform the student or students in advance of the upcoming test date.

_____ Thoroughly read the examiner's manual of the test to be administered.

_____ Check and assemble all test materials. Test materials could possibly include:

- #2 pencils
- Stop Watch
- Student Booklets
- Examiner's Manual
- Scratch Paper
- Calculators
- *Testing—Do Not Disturb* Sign

_____ Select and reserve testing location. The test location should be comfortable and free from distractions.

_____ Review the examiner's manual the day before testing and highlight important notes or items in the directions. In addition, colored adhesive tabs can be placed in the examiner's manual to mark each section of the test.

_____ Other: _____

_____

During the Test

_____ Post the *Testing—Do Not Disturb* sign on the outside of the door of test location.

_____ Request students to sign in if testing in a large group.

_____ Distribute test materials to students.

_____ Read the test directions to students.

_____ Write the start time of the test in a highly visible location when testing a large group.

_____ Monitor students.

_____ Other: _____

_____

(Continued)

Form 7.1 (Continued)

After the Test

_____ Collect all test materials carefully and promptly.

_____ Collect pencils, scratch paper, or other materials given to students for testing purposes.

_____ Remove testing sign from door.

_____ Return to classroom and count test materials.

_____ Place order to replenish test materials.

_____ Store all tests in a secure location until they can be sent for scoring or the teacher arranges to score the test.

_____ Write formal report on test results.

_____ Other: _____

_____

_____

Resource 7.1   Educational Assessments

The following is an overview of various assessments the first-year special education teacher may encounter at some point during his or her career. Some of the tests listed below are utilized in identifying students with disabilities, while others can be utilized to measure student progress. The list is only a sampling of the multitude of assessments that are in existence.

- ***AAMR Adaptive Behavior Scale–School, Second Edition**
  Author: Nadine Lambert, Kazuo Nihira, and Henry Leland
  Purpose: "Used to assess adaptive behavior."

- ****Bender Visual Motor Gestalt Test, Second Edition**
  Author: Lauretta Bender
  Age-group: All ages
  Purpose: "Assess the visual-motor functions of individuals from age three years to adulthood. Also used in the evaluation of developmental problems in children, learning disabilities, retardation, psychosis, and organic brain disorders." (p. 37)

- ***California Achievement Tests, Fifth Edition**
  Author: CTB Macmillan/McGraw-Hill
  Purpose: "Designed to measure achievement in the basic skills taught in schools throughout the nation."

- ***Criterion Test of Basic Skills [2000 Edition]**
  Author: Keith Lundell, William Brown, and James Evans
  Purpose: "Developed to assess the basic reading and arithmetic skills of individual students."

- ***Differential Aptitude Tests, Fifth Edition**
  Author: G. K. Bennett, H. G. Seashore, and A. G. Wesman
  Purpose: "Designed to measure students' ability to learn or to succeed in a number of different areas."

- ***House-Tree-Person and Draw-A-Person as Measure of Abuse in Children: A Quantitative Scoring System**
  Author: Valerie Van Hutton
  Purpose: "Developed to assess personality/emotional characteristics of sexually abused children."

- ***Iowa Tests of Basic Skills(r), Forms K, L, and M**
  Author: H. D. Hoover, A. N. Hieronymous, D. A. Frisbie, and S. B. Dunbar
  Purpose: "To provide a comprehensive assessment of student progress in the basic skills."

- ***The Minnesota Multiphasic Personality Inventory–2**
  Author: James N. Butcher, W. Grant Dahlstrom, John R. Graham,
  Auke Tellegen, and Beverly Kaemmer
  Purpose: "Designed to assess a number of the major patterns of personality and emotional disorders."

(Continued)

Resource 7.1 (Continued)

- ***The Minnesota Multiphasic Personality Inventory–Adolescent**
  Author: James N. Butcher, Carolyn L. Williams, John R. Graham,
  Beverly Kaemmer, Robert P. Archer, Auke Tellegen, and Yossef S. Ben-Porath
  Purpose: Designed for use with adolescents to assess a number of the major patterns of personality and emotional disorders.

- ***Otis-Lennon School Ability Test, Seventh Edition**
  Author: Arthur S. Otis and Roger T. Lennon
  Purpose: "Designed to measure abstract thinking and reasoning ability."

- ***Peabody Individual Achievement Test–Revised [1998 Normative Update]**
  Author: Frederick C. Markwardt, Jr.
  Purpose: Designed to measure academic achievement.

- ***Peabody Picture Vocabulary Test–III**
  Author: Lloyd M. Dunn, Leota M. Dunn, Kathleen T. Williams, and Jing-Jen Wang
  Purpose: Designed to measure receptive vocabulary; can also be used as a screening test of verbal ability.

- ***Rotter Incomplete Sentences Blank, Second Edition**
  Author: Julian B. Rotter, Michael I. Lah, and Janet E. Rafferty
  Purpose: Primarily used "as a screening instrument of overall adjustment."

- ***Scales for Diagnosing Attention-Deficit/Hyperactivity Disorder**
  Author: Gail Ryser and Kathleen McConnell
  Purpose: "To help identify children and adolescents who have attention-difficulty/hyperactivity disorder (ADHD)."

- ***Slosson Full-Range Intelligence Test**
  Author: Bob Algozzine, Ronald C. Eaves, Lester Mann, and H. Robert Vance
  Editor: Steven W. Slosson
  Purpose: Constructed as a "quick estimate of general cognitive ability."

- ***Stanford-Binet Intelligence Scale, Fourth Edition**
  Author: Robert L. Thorndike, Elizabeth P. Hagen, Jerome M. Sattler,
  Elizabeth A. Delaney, and Thomas F. Hopkins
  Purpose: Designed as "an instrument for measuring cognitive abilities that provides an analysis of pattern as well as the overall level of an individual's cognitive development."

- ****Stanford Measurement Series–Stanford Achievement Test: 7th Edition**
  Author: Eric F. Gardner, Herbert C. Rudman, Bjorn Karlsen, and Jack Merwin
  Age-group: Grades 1.5–9.9
  Purpose: Assess school achievement status of children from first through tenth grade (p. 396).

- ***Test of Nonverbal Intelligence, Third Edition**
  Author: Linda Brown, Rita J. Sherbenou, and Susan K. Johnsen
  Purpose: "Developed to assess aptitude, intelligence, abstract reasoning, and problem solving in a completely language-free format."

- ***Test of Written Language–Third Edition**
  Author: Donald D. Hammill and Stephen C. Larsen
  Purpose: Designed to "(a) identify students who perform significantly more poorly than their peers in writing and who as a result need special help; (b) determine a student's particular strengths and weaknesses in various writing abilities; (c) document a student's progress in a special writing program; and conduct research in writing."

- ***Vineland Adaptive Behavior Scales**
  Author: Sara S. Sparrow, David A. Balla, Domenic V. Cicchetti, and Patti L. Harrison
  Purpose: To "assess personal and social sufficiency of individuals from birth to adulthood."

- ***Wechsler Intelligence Scale for Children–Third Edition**
  Author: David Wechsler
  Purpose: A "measure of a child's intellectual ability."

- ***Wide Range Achievement Test 3**
  Author: Gary S. Wilkinson
  Purpose: To measure the skills needed to learn reading, spelling, and arithmetic.

---

*SOURCE: *Buros Institute of Mental Measurement Test Reviews Online.* (n.d.). Retrieved April 23, 2004, from http://buros.unl.edu/buros/jsp/reviews.jsp?item=06000003.

**SOURCE: Sweetland, R. C., & O'Connor, W. (Eds.). (1984). *Tests: A comprehensive reference for assessments in psychology, education and business.* Kansas City, MO: SKS Associates.

Resource 7.2 Possible Modifications for Students With Disabilities

The Florida Department of Education has identified the following possible modifications for IEP teams to consider for students with disabilities. The reader should utilize the information only as a guide when developing appropriate modifications for individual students.

- *Flexible Setting*

  Students may take an assessment individually or in a small group setting under a proctor's supervision. Lighting, acoustics, adaptive or special furniture, and distraction-free locations are flexible-setting situations for consideration.

- *Flexible Scheduling*

  Students may take the test during several brief sessions within one school day. More frequent or extended breaks may be needed. The test may be administered at a time of day that is most beneficial to the student. Test proctors may need to encourage students to answer one type of test question first and then others (e.g., multiple choice may be easier for a particular student than extended response questions).

- *Flexible Timing*

  Students may be provided additional time. Caution should be taken in automatically providing extended time. Test proctors should carefully monitor the use of time by students. Extended testing time may only prolong test anxiety for some students; test proctors should be attuned to the needs of each student using modifications. Students who are testing with Braille or large print versions generally benefit from the use of extended time because of the reduced reading speed typically associated with the use of these formats.

- *Flexible Presentation*

  Students may use mechanical aids such as a magnifying device, a pointer, a template, or other similar device to assist in maintaining visual attention to the test items. Directions and items not assessing reading may be read to students. Directions may be reread, paraphrased, or simplified. It may be helpful for students to restate the directions in their own words. Test proctors may need to color code the instructions to help emphasize the steps. Other presentation considerations include reading or signing directions, writing prompts, or math items to students; turning the pages for the student; allowing the teacher who typically works with the student to administer the test; assisting the student with moving from one item to another; and encouragement by test proctor to begin, keep going, or stay on task without affecting the student's choice of responses on the test.

- *Flexible Responding*

  Students may provide an oral response, a signed response, a response on a word processor, or a response on a Braillewriter. If an oral response is given by a student on the Florida Writing Assessment, the student must indicate punctuation. Directions for transcribing oral, signed, or word-processed responses are indicated in the testing instructions available from the district test coordinator. Student responses must not be edited when transcribed. Other flexible responding considerations include allowing the student to write in the test booklet or allowing the student to use special paper (lined or gridded).

SOURCE: Florida Department of Education, Division of Public Schools and Community Education, Bureau of Instructional Support and Community Services. Technical assistance paper, *Guidelines for Determining Modifications for Use on State and District Assessments for Students With Disabilities.* Tallahasee, FL: Author.

Writing Legal and Effective Individualized Education Programs

The principle goal of education is to create men who are capable of doing new things, not simply of repeating what other generations have done— men who are creative, inventive and discoverers.

—Jean Piaget

The writing of an Individualized Education Program (IEP) for a student with a disability is one of the most important tasks the first-year special education teacher will undertake during the school year. The IEP is a legal document that is mandated by the Individuals with Disabilities Education Act (IDEA) and initially developed after the student is found to be eligible for services. A team of individuals are required to meet and review the student's IEP each year and upon the completion of a 3-year reevaluation. The purpose of the annual review meeting is to evaluate the success of current instructional strategies, annotate the completion of current goals and objectives, and develop a solid plan designed to address the educational needs of the student. The IEP can be revised or revisited at any time, and the authors recommend that the special education teacher review the plan throughout the year to chart student progress and note significant problem areas. If the educational strategies, current placement, or any other factor in the plan appear to be ineffective, the teacher should organize a team meeting and make the appropriate adjustments to the student's IEP. According to the regulations, the IEP team must be composed of a general education teacher if the student is currently participating in a general classroom setting or possibly will at a future date, a school administrator or someone who has knowledge of the general curriculum, representatives of outside public agencies, individuals qualified to supervise the implementation of the IEP, the parents of the student, and the student when deemed appropriate. Other individuals may participate as part of the IEP team at the parents' discretion. Tremendous amounts of time and skill are involved in writing a plan that can meet the legal requirements or mandates and that effectively communicates the needs of the student. The plan serves as the instructional blueprint for special and general education teachers.

The authors have identified three basic skills that the special education teacher should possess before writing his or her first IEP of the school year. First, the new teacher must have a clear understanding of the IDEA rules and regulations that specifically address the content of the IEP before attempting to write his or her first document of the school year. The essential information that every IEP is legally required to contain is specifically stated in Section 300.347 of the rules and regulations. The components that compose the section address the following: information pertaining to the child's present levels of performance; how deficits will be addressed and progress measured; the need for specific special education services, related services, and supplementary aids; the extent the child with a disability will participate with nondisabled students during the school day; testing modifications; the projected start and end dates of a child's IEP; how the student is progressing toward the annual goals; how the parents were informed; and transition services. In this chapter, the authors provide the teacher with a summary and reference for each component. The authors focus on the content aspect of the IEP to assist the new special education teacher in writing a plan that will survive a due process hearing. Next, the special education teacher must possess the ability to communicate all student information accurately and succinctly to write an effective IEP. The teacher should use language that can be easily understood by most audiences; provide information that is of an objective nature; and formulate an overall plan of action that can easily be followed by special and general education teachers, support personnel, and parents. The plan should be written on a personal level with positive overtones. Finally, the beginning teacher must establish and maintain rapport with parents and students to promote their active involvement in the IEP process. The authors provide the teacher with tips on how to increase the participation of students and parents and focus the importance of their roles in the development of a solid IEP. Parental support is critical to a student's success in the school setting.

The chapter is structured in a format that will enlighten the teacher as to the legal aspects of the IEP and assist with writing of an effective plan. The authors have included an IEP conference checklist (Form 8.1, p. 147), facts pertaining to the No Child Left Behind Act (Resource 8.1, p. 149) and Improving Education Results for Children with Disabilities Act (Resource 8.2, p. 150), and sources for computer software programs to assist with the writing of IEPs (Resource 8.3, p. 152). The authors encourage the reader to use only forms and documents that have been approved by his or her school system when conducting IEP meetings. In addition, the teacher must be familiar with his or her state laws that govern the education of students with disabilities.

SECTION 1: THE LEGAL REQUIREMENTS OF AN IEP

The first-year teacher should have a clear understanding of the current federal rules and regulations contained in the IDEA that specifically address the content of the IEP before attempting to write his or her first document. The essential information that every IEP is legally required to contain is specifically stated in Section 300.347 of the IDEA rules and regulations. The information in this section was obtained from the *Federal Register*, Volume 64, Number 48 (March 12, 1999). The authors strongly encourage the reader to obtain all updates of this information from his or her special education director or the U.S. Department of Education on a yearly basis. The law is currently up for reauthorization, but no action had been taken as of the publishing of this handbook.

- Present Levels of Performance[1]

  1. A statement of the child's present levels of educational performance, including
     (i) How the child's disability affects the child's involvement and progress in the general curriculum (i.e., the same curriculum as for nondisabled children); or
     (ii) For preschool children, as appropriate, how the disability affects the child's participation in appropriate activities.

- Statement of Annual Goals and Benchmarks or Objectives

  2. A statement of measurable annual goals, including benchmarks or short-term objectives, related to
     (i) Meeting the child's needs that result from the child's disability to enable the child to be involved in and progress in the general curriculum (i.e., the same curriculum as for nondisabled children), or for preschool children, as appropriate, to participate in appropriate activities; and
     (ii) Meeting each of the child's other educational needs that result from the child's disability.

- Statement of Services, Supplementary Aids, and Program Modifications or Supports

  3. A statement of the special education and related services and supplementary aids and services to be provided to the child, or on behalf of the child, and a statement of the program modifications or supports for school personnel that will be provided for the child
     (i) To advance appropriately toward attaining the annual goals;
     (ii) To be involved and progress in the general curriculum in accordance with paragraph (a) (1) of this section and to participate in extracurricular and other nonacademic activities; and
     (iii) To be educated and participate with other children with disabilities and nondisabled children in the activities described in this section.

- Student Placement in Academic, Extracurricular, and Nonacademic Activities

  4. An explanation of the extent, if any, to which the child will not participate with nondisabled children in the regular class and in the activities described in paragraph (3).

- Student Assessment Modifications

  5. (i) A statement of any individual modifications in the administration of state or districtwide assessments of student achievement that are needed for the child to participate in the assessment; and
  (ii) if the IEP team determines that the child will not participate in a particular state or districtwide assessment of student achievement (or part of an assessment), a statement of
      A. Why that assessment is not appropriate for the child; and
      B. How the child will be assessed.

- Student Service Dates, Frequency, Location, Duration, and Program Modifications

  6. The projected date for the beginning of the services and modifications and the anticipated frequency, location, and duration of those services and modifications.

- Student Progress: Measuring, Evaluating, and Informing Parents

  7. A statement of
  (i) How the child's progress toward the annual goals will be measured; and
  (ii) How the child's parents will be regularly informed (through such means as periodic report cards), at least as often as parents are informed of their nondisabled children's progress, of
      A. Their child's progress toward the annual goals; and
      B. The extent to which that progress is sufficient to enable the child to achieve the goals by the end of the year.

- Transition Services

  The IEP must include

  1. For each student with a disability beginning at age 14 (or younger if determined appropriate by the IEP team), and updated annually, a statement of the transition service needs of the student under the applicable components of the student's IEP that focuses on the student's courses of study (such as participation in advanced placement courses or a vocational education program); and

  2. For each student beginning at age 16 (or younger, if determined appropriate by the IEP team), a statement of needed transition services for the student, including, if appropriate, a statement of the interagency responsibilities or any needed linkages.

- Transfer of Rights

In a state that transfers rights at the age of majority, beginning at least 1 year before a student reaches the age of majority under state law, the student's IEP must include a statement that the student has been informed of his or her rights under Part B of the act, if any, that will transfer to the student on reaching the age of majority, consistent with Section 300.517.

---

[1]SOURCE: Authority: 20 U.S.C. 1414(d)(1)(A) and (d)(6)(A)(ii).

SECTION 2: UNDERSTANDING THE COMPONENTS OF AN IEP

Present Level of Performance

The authors view the present level of educational performance as one of the most important components of the IEP. In this section, an educational profile of the student is developed with input from the IEP team. The profile should provide the reader with a comprehensive perspective of the student and provide the framework for the other IEP components. The present level of education performance is typically written in a narrative format and can be easily read by parents, students, and other professionals. The teacher is encouraged to write in nontechnical language and use the student's first name when appropriate. This will improve the readability and personalize the document. The authors consider the following information to be crucial to produce the present levels of educational performance component of the IEP. The special education teacher should write specific statements that address each area listed (as appropriate):

- Current test/evaluation data
- Vision and hearing screening
- Student achievement
- Communication skills
- Strengths and weaknesses (e.g., reading comprehension and impulse control)
- Social adaptation skills
- Fine and gross motor skills
- Psychomotor skills
- Review student progress in the special education classroom
- Review student progress in the general education classroom

Annual Goals and Objectives or Benchmarks

Annual goals are statements that address the student's areas of weakness that were identified in the present levels of performance section of the IEP. The goals should generally state what the student will be able to do by the end date of the IEP. For example,

- Susan will be able to complete a simple job application form.
- Susan will increase her reading comprehension skills.

An *objective* is a description of a performance one wants learners to be able to exhibit before one considers them competent. An objective describes an intended result of instruction rather than a process of instruction (Mager, 1984, p. 5). Objectives support the annual goals and must be measurable. A good objective will specifically state what the learner is to do, under what conditions the performance will occur, and the quality level of the performance. Remember that every objective must have a review date, method of evaluation, and criteria for mastery. For example,

- Given the personal information section on a simple job application, the student will complete the section with less that five errors.
- Given a selected story in the student's basal reader, the student will read the story silently and then answer four out of five comprehension questions correctly.

Services, Supplementary Aids, and Program Modifications or Supports

- Special education services: State specific special education program and environment in which the student will be serviced
- Related services areas: occupational therapy, physical therapy, adaptive PE, special and regular transportation, counseling services, and so on

Student Placement: Academic, Extracurricular, and Nonacademic Activities

- Academic: core curriculum area, exploratory, specialty, or elective classes
- Extracurricular: clubs, athletic teams, cheerleading, and so on
- Nonacademic: lunch, recess, assemblies, and so on

Individual Modifications for Student Achievement Assessments

- Special education students must be assessed during the school year.
- The IEP team must state an alternative assessment method if the student is not going to participate in the statewide testing program.
- IDEA '97 allows for reasonable test accommodations. Examples of acceptable test accommodations for standardized tests are as follows:
  a. Small-group testing
  b. Individual testing
  c. Read test to student
  d. Provide alternative response methods
  e. Test in a room with carpet
  f. Provide student with a study carrel

Service Dates, Frequency, Location, Duration, and Program Modifications

- Specifically state the exact start and end dates of the IEP.
- The IEP should list the school or facility location.
- Frequency and duration indicate "how often and for how long."
- Program modifications refer to the adaptations the teacher is implementing for the student to be successful in the classroom.

Student Progress: Measuring, Evaluating, Informing Parents, and Transition Services

- Examples of measurement and evaluation tools are teacher-made tests, textbook unit tests, standardized tests, behavior rating scale, class point system, and teacher observation.
- Informing parents: Parents should be informed via school report card, school progress report, weekly progress report, telephone, and parent-teacher conferences.
- A transition plan must be developed for students age 14. A good transition plan will address the student's needs, interests, and aptitudes. Transition activities include community, daily living, and employment experiences. Transition plans should address high school programs of study and postsecondary options for older students.

SECTION 3: INVOLVING STUDENTS AND PARENTS IN THE IEP PROCESS

The involvement of students (at the appropriate age) and parents in the IEP process is mandated by IDEA; their active participation as team members is critical to the success of the IEP. The authors have found that the following strategies increase the active participation of parents in the IEP process:

- Establish a working relationship or rapport with parents prior to any mandatory meetings.
- Establish and maintain an open line of communication with parents throughout the school year.
- Personally call to arrange the IEP meeting at a date and time convenient for the parents, and follow up with the required written notification.
- The IEP meeting should be held in a location that is comfortable and free of distractions.
- The seating arrangement should be in a manner that projects the feeling of equity among the team members (use a round table instead of a rectangular one).
- Team members should use language throughout the conference that is simplistic and free of professional jargon.
- Team members should listen to parent concerns or comments or both and encourage parents to be active participants throughout the conference.

- Ensure that the parents leave the conference with an understanding of the plan for their child and confident that all plans will be carried out by all designated individuals.
- Follow up with parents a few days after the meeting to check for any additional questions or concerns.

The new teacher will find that encouraging students, who are of the appropriate age, to become active participants in the process is a more challenging task. Older students are often unclear as to their current status and the entire IEP concept. The authors suggest involving the student in the planning of the IEP meeting date and discussing all information that will be reviewed during the time period. During their search for effective strategies to promote student involvement, the authors discovered the concept of "student-led IEPs." Mason, McGahee-Kovac, and Johnson (2004) found the following:

> Process-student-led IEPs teach students to take ownership for their own education and to demonstrate that ownership at an annual IEP meeting. Through our research on student-led IEPs, we found that students and teachers alike reported that students using this process knew more about their disabilities, legal rights, and appropriate accommodations than other students and that students gained increased self-confidence and the ability to advocate for themselves. (p. 18)

The student-led IEP has three levels of student involvement, and the students receive training in the IEP process from the special education teacher. The culminating activity is when the student actually conducts the IEP conference. Although the authors are unclear as to the legal and ethical issues surrounding the concept, this is definitely an "out-of-the-box" idea and one worth a second look.

Form 8.1   Essential Information for the Annual Individual Education Program
Conference

Directions: The special education teacher must review his or her school district's policies
regarding IEP conferences and use only approved special education forms for all formal
IEP meetings. The following information must be collected and reviewed by the special
education teacher prior to the annual IEP conference. All collected documentation
should be shared with the parents in advance of the scheduled meeting.

_____ **Review Current Levels of Performance**

1. Educational assessments
   a. Intelligence
   b. Academic achievement
   c. Learning style
   d. Adaptive behavior
   e. Social/emotional
   f. Fine and gross motor

2. Audiology assessment

3. Speech/language pathologist assessment

4. Physical therapy assessment

5. Occupational therapy assessment

6. Fine and gross motor skills assessment

7. Current medical status

_____ **Review Current Individualized Education Program**

1. Goals and objectives (annotate the mastered goals and objectives on current IEP)

2. Related services: transportation, physical therapy, occupational therapy, speech
   and language therapy, other

3. Student's current placement
   _____ Regular class
   _____ Separate/self-contained class
   _____ Private separate school facility
   _____ Private residential facility
   _____ Resource class
   _____ Public separate school facility
   _____ Public residential facility
   _____ Homebound/hospital environment

4. Student's discipline plan

5. Student's behavior management plan

6. Student's standardized testing modifications

7. Student's transition plan

(Continued)

Form 8.1 (Continued)

_____ **Review Student's Performance in Regular Education Classes**

_____ Test grades

_____ Quiz grades

_____ Academic portfolio

_____ Homework completion

_____ Class participation

_____ On-task behavior

_____ Conduct

_____ **Review General Student Information**

_____ Attendance record

_____ Discipline record

_____ School transcript (high school students only)

_____ Student program of study (high school students only)

Resource 8.1   Facts Pertaining to the No Child Left Behind Act

- The cornerstone of the No Child Left Behind Act (NCLB), signed into law by President Bush on January 8, 2002, is improving results for all students, including those with special needs.

- Under NCLB, schools, school districts, and states are asked to show progress in educating children with special needs. If expectations are not met, both parents and schools qualify for emergency help. Schools qualify for extra funding and technical assistance. Parents of children with special needs in underachieving schools are given new options, including the option of sending their children to higher-achieving public schools or charter schools and the option of obtaining supplemental educational services such as private tutoring for their children.

- Parents of children with special needs receive report cards on school achievement in special education as well as other academic areas. These report cards will enhance parents' ability to make informed choices about their children's education.

- Parents of children with special needs will have access to information that lets them know whether their children are learning from a highly qualified teacher.

- NCLB requires that all children with special needs attending federally funded schools have the opportunity to learn from a highly qualified special education teacher. States must submit a plan to ensure all teachers teaching special education are highly qualified by the end of the 2005–2006 school year.

- Under NCLB, federally funded schools that have not made adequate yearly progress (as defined by the state) for special education for 2 consecutive years will be identified by the state or district as needing improvement. If a school is identified as needing improvement, both the school and the parents of children with special needs attending that school qualify for emergency help.

- Parents of children with special needs receive the option of sending their children to another public school or charter school immediately (with priority given to those students who are low achieving or low income). In addition, if a school continues to underachieve, parents of children with special needs may obtain supplemental educational services for their children—including tutoring, after-school services, and summer school programs—using a portion of their children's share of federal Title I funds (again based on priority for those students who are low achieving or low income).

- NCLB allows 20% of funds allocated to states under Reading First to be used specifically for the professional development of teachers, including special education teachers. One goal of the professional development activities is to help special education teachers provide reading instruction to students with special needs. In many instances, special education classes are filled with children who were simply never taught to read. This funding will provide teachers with the instruction needed to get these kids caught up in reading and out of the special education system, where they never belonged.

SOURCE: Committee on Education and the Workforce, U.S. House of Representatives, http://www.mla.org.

Resource 8.2   Facts Pertaining to the Improving Education Results for the Children with Disabilities Act

- On March 19, 2003, U.S. House Education & the Workforce Committee members, led by Education Reform Subcommittee Chairman Mike Castle (R-DE), introduced the Improving Education Results for Children with Disabilities Act (H.R. 1350). This legislation would make several significant reforms to the nation's special education law, the Individuals with Disabilities Education Act (IDEA), including an increased focus on academic results for children with disabilities and a reduction in the paperwork burden overwhelming schools and driving much-needed teachers out of the classroom.

- The act is the product of an extensive series of hearings and more than 1 year of input from teachers, parents, and those involved with special education.

- Proposals such as the 3-year IEP provide options for states and parents—options parents and paperwork-weary teachers alike believe the law should allow for students with disabilities. If parents prefer to have an annual IEP, the law guarantees that right. The 3-year IEP, if agreed to by the parents and the school, would maintain critical individualized education to children with special needs while reducing complex and duplicative paperwork. Furthermore, if parents decide the 3-year IEP is not working, they can simply ask to return to the annual IEP—and they do not have to wait until the 3-year IEP is completed.

- The elimination of benchmarks and short-term objectives will not take effect until the 2005–2006 school year because, beginning in 2005, all parents will receive report cards from schools showing academic progress indicators. Until that time, IEPs will continue to contain short-term objectives and benchmarks to ensure academic progress is being made. After that time, those students who are being assessed using alternate assessment may continue to have benchmarks and short-term objectives.

- The discipline provisions contained in the bill ensure that no child is left behind. In fact, the bill explicitly guarantees that children with disabilities will continue to receive educational services regardless of any disciplinary action taken. Under current law, discipline procedures for children with disabilities and nondisabled children can be significantly different, even for serious offenses such as bringing a weapon to school. This is unfair to teachers, students, and even children with disabilities. The proposal in H.R. 1350 would allow schools, at their discretion and with the ability to consider all circumstances including a disability, to assign the same punishment for disabled and nondisabled children. Even in the case of suspension, however, a child with a disability would continue to receive educational services to ensure progress is made on an IEP. This improves safety for schools while ensuring protections for children with special needs.

- The changes in the complaint process proposed in H.R. 1350 are designed to improve communication, restore trust, and strengthen cooperation between parents and school personnel. By providing options such as binding arbitration, parents and schools will have new opportunities to address problems without fear of costly litigation. In fact, changes to the procedural safeguard provisions maintain every civil rights protection for children and families while going a step further to provide optional, alternative means of dispute resolution that will only improve effective communication and cooperation among parents, teachers, and schools.

- The 1-year statute of limitations proposed in H.R. 1350 is a protection for both parents and schools that will help ensure the timely resolution of complaints. Reforms to the complaint process will help restore trust and allow teachers to feel confident that they can teach without fear of frivolous litigation that could jeopardize educational opportunities for other children with disabilities. The rights of parents are preserved under H.R. 1350, but innovative solutions are proposed to resolve problems in a timely fashion, reduce costly litigation, and refocus IDEA on teaching children rather than compliance with regulations.

SOURCE: Committee on Education and the Workforce, U.S. House of Representatives, http://www.mla.org.

Resource 8.3   IEP Software Programs to Assist the Special Education Teacher

- **CEC Satellite Broadcast: Choosing Your IEP Software**
  www.cec.sped.org/pd/janiep.html

- **CLASS IEP Program**
  www.classplus.com/contact.htm

- **IEP Software**
  www.orionsystems.com

- **IEP TeamWare—Special Education IEP Software**
  www.teacherspetproductions.com/ieptw.html

- **Individual Education Plan (IEP) Software**
  www.iepware.com

- **Interactive IEP Internet**
  www.specialsolutions.com/iep.html

- **Links, Horizon Software Systems, Inc. Special Education IEP**
  www.excent.com/News/links.htm

- **Netchemia Internet Solutions for the Americas**
  www.netchemia.com/Services/netIEP.asp

- **PennStar IEP software**
  www.diskbooks.org/pstar.html

- **Teacher's Choice IEP Software**
  www.db-es.com/product3.htm

Preparing Students for Transition

The most important thing that parents can teach their children is how to get along without them.

—Frank A. Clark, 1911

According to Kohler and Field (2003), "Transition to adult roles can be a complicated process, one that all youths must negotiate, and a myriad of factors work together to affect students' lives after school completion" (p. 181). Most people "transition" at approximately age 5 or 6 to public school; exit school at approximately age 18 to the post-school life options of work, marriage, college, or the military; and many retire at approximately age 62. Wehman (1996) has found that planning for transitions at all ages promotes the social and emotional well-being of students with disabilities. Planning for major life transitions, such as enrollment in full-day public school and the change from school to post-school, is mandated by the Individuals with Disabilities Education Act (IDEA). Any change in a student's schedule, placement, school, or even transportation, however, should be viewed as an opportunity to help the student prepare for future transition experiences. The special education teacher, along with the Individualized Education Program (IEP) team, is responsible for developing effective plans to prepare students for a variety of transitions ranging from changing schools to pursuing post-school endeavors. The role of the special education teacher is to provide students with strategies that will lay the foundation for successful transition experiences and to facilitate students' explorations of possibilities for post-school options and the setting of realistic career goals with each student's strengths, challenges, interests, and abilities in mind. The transition planning process provides an excellent opportunity to increase the self-advocacy and self-determination skills of students as they prepare for adulthood. Many students with disabilities have traditionally not been afforded the same number of opportunities to make decisions and choices as students without disabilities. Empowering students to be self-directed should be the ultimate goal of the special education teacher, and working with the student on transition planning can help to empower the student.

In this chapter, three strategies are presented that will assist the new teacher in his or her efforts to prepare students for transition. The strategies involve providing an overview of the IDEA rules and regulations pertaining to the transition of students with disabilities and assisting students with two common transitional issues. These issues revolve around the movement of students with disabilities to a new school and to post-school experiences. The authors acknowledge that a tremendous amount of diversity exists among students with disabilities; the ultimate goal of the special education teacher, however, must be to assist each student in developing the essential skills necessary to meet the challenges of independent living. Supplemental forms and resource information designed to assist the new teacher in preparing students for transitional experiences are provided at the end of the chapter.

STRATEGY 1: UNDERSTAND THE LEGAL ASPECTS OF TRANSITION

All students with IEPs must have Individual Transition Plans (ITPs) by the age of 14 or the end of the eighth grade. The content of the ITP must address post-school desires and needs of the student. The plan must be reviewed annually, and the present level of performance, the goals, and the objectives should be focused on post-school outcomes. The student and any community agency personnel involved in transition planning, such as a vocational rehabilitation counselor, must be involved in the annual ITP meeting. Some school districts develop ITPs separately from IEPs. Others incorporate the transition plan into the student's IEP. Teachers should contact their local school district for specific guidelines.

Existing requirements were expanded in IDEA '97 for the IEP to include transition service needs (beginning at age 14 and updated annually) that focus on the student's courses of study. This should include, when appropriate, the interagency responsibilities or needed linkages (beginning at age 16 or younger) and a statement that the child has been informed of the rights that will transfer to him or her on reaching the age of majority ("A Primer on IDEA," 1999). For example, students planning to attend college should be informed of their rights to modifications in college or technical school classrooms under the Americans with Disabilities Act (Public Law 101-336).

STRATEGY 2: PREPARE STUDENTS FOR MOVEMENT TO A NEW SCHOOL

Changing schools can be a very traumatic event for students with disabilities. Going from elementary to middle school and from middle to high school both involve several adjustments. For example, a child transitioning from a half-day preschool program to full-day first grade may need to prepare for navigating the lunchroom, playground, media center, or other new physical environments as well as classroom skills such as sitting at a desk, raising one's hand to be called on, following instructions, taking turns, and walking down the hall in line. Students' concerns or issues vary depending on the grade level. Queen (2002) found that students transitioning from middle school to high school often have concerns pertaining to

- Being tardy to class (getting to class on time), finding lockers, crowded hallways, and getting lost
- Being victimized or harassed by others or both
- Being safe at school
- Being able to understand difficult classes
- Coping with rigid rules and strict teachers
- Being able to make new friends in a new setting (p. 21)

Next, several suggestions to prepare students for a positive transition experience are discussed.

Suggestion 1: Conduct the Annual IEP Meeting at the New School

The IEP of each student is required to be reviewed on an annual basis. The authors suggest that the student's annual review meeting be held at the new school. This is a prime opportunity for the parents and student to meet the new special education teacher and ask the multitude of questions that typically accompany this type of transition. The meeting also provides the new teacher an opportunity to begin building rapport with the family, which is the key element to a successful partnership between home and school. In addition, the authors strongly urge the teachers from both schools to communicate on a regular basis to promote program continuity and maintain a clear understanding of the student expectations for the next level.

Suggestion 2: Create an Information Booklet

A primer or simple booklet providing useful information pertaining to the new school for students and parents given out well in advance of the change can be very helpful. Booklets may include information that is school specific, such as a school calendar, bell schedule, absence policy, dress code, code of conduct, extracurricular activities, and graduation requirements. The teacher may also use the booklet to provide information that is specific to his or her classroom or program and to highlight classroom policies and procedures, expectations, required student materials, and teacher contact information. The authors suggest including a list of the most common questions asked by parents and students and providing a response to each somewhere in the booklet.

Suggestion 3: Provide a Private Orientation of the New School

Another helpful idea is for the parents and students to visit the new school to become familiar with the physical layout of the building. The orientation should include a school tour, an introduction to all special education staff members, and an overview of important school policies and procedures. The authors recommend that the special education teacher have the schedules of all students who will be mainstreamed or served in inclusion settings available for students and parents to preview and find the locations of these classes. If the orientation session is offered during the day, this is a great opportunity for students and parents to meet school staff members, such as the principal, secretaries, and custodians.

STRATEGY 3: PREPARE STUDENTS FOR POST-SCHOOL ENDEAVORS

The transition of students with disabilities to post-school experiences is typically filled with an array of emotions for students and parents. The time has finally arrived, and students must move to the next phase of their lives. The special education teacher must develop strategies designed to assist, facilitate, and promote the smooth transition of high school students to the next level of education or direct entry into the modern workforce. Students who plan to enter postsecondary institutions need assistance in setting goals, developing study and time management skills, achieving in high-level academic courses, and obtaining the academic skills necessary to become independent learners. Students who will enter directly into the modern workforce after high school need assistance in developing minimum entry-level skills to successfully gain employment. The authors present several suggestions to prepare students for post-school endeavors.

Suggestion 1: Focus on Career Development

The beginning teacher should integrate career development activities into his or her program or academic curriculum to promote career awareness and employment readiness skills with all students regardless of disability. The activities should be appropriate for the age and level of functioning of each student. The new teacher should assist students in answering the following questions, which are critical to the career development process: Who am I? Where am I going? How am I going to get there? Next, the teacher should assist students in identifying their personal abilities, interests, and values in terms of work and then in developing a career goal that does not conflict with this information. Finally, the new teacher must assist students in acquiring the necessary knowledge and the application of skills that are necessary for achieving identified career goals. The authors encourage the beginning teacher to enlist the assistance of the school counselor when developing his or her career activities.

Suggestion 2: Assist Students in Meeting the Requirements for Admission Into Postsecondary Institutions

Students who have a desire to attend postsecondary institutions (technical colleges and 2- and 4-year colleges or universities) upon graduation from high school must possess the academic skills to gain entrance and survive in the higher-education environment. The special education teacher must ensure that the students on his or her caseload who plan to attend college are placed into high school programs of studies that will prepare them for the rigor of college. The teacher should work closely with the school counselor to ensure that each student's course selections and standardized test scores meet the minimum requirements for his or her college selection. The authors have created a High School 4-Year Plan form that the teacher can use to assist students and their parents in designing a high school plan that is appropriate for students pursuing a college education after graduation. The authors have also included a Unit-Credit Checklist form that the teacher can use to not only monitor his or her students' progress toward meeting high school graduation requirements but also to ensure that students are following their high school plan. Finally, students and parents typically have numerous questions regarding the services that will be available to students with disabilities at the postsecondary institution. The U.S Department of Education Office for Civil Rights has published a booklet that addresses these questions. The authors provide selections from the booklet at the end of the chapter so that the new teacher can assist parents in finding answers to their questions.

Materials or Resources

Form 9.1: High School 4-Year Plan

Form 9.2: Unit of Credit Checklist

Resource 9.1: Students With Disabilities Preparing for Postsecondary Education: Know Your Rights and Responsibilities

Suggestion 3: Focus on Work-Based Skills

The authors recommend that high school special education teachers working with students who are in the mild to moderate range of intellectual functioning develop an academic program that focuses on work-based skills. Typically, the students in this range of functioning are capable of acquiring the skills necessary to meet the challenges of independent living and working to some degree. The program should have a school-to-career focus and provide students with supervised work experiences designed to teach employability skills; gain job- or site-specific skills; foster work-oriented relationships with adults; and enable pupils to acquire attitudes, skills, and knowledge of life roles in real work settings. The teacher will find that despite his or her best efforts, there will be some students who require lifelong supervision; in keeping with the ultimate goal of transition, however, a work-based program will promote the skills necessary for independent living. The authors recommend several steps for developing a work-based education program for students with mild to moderate disabilities.

Step 1: Develop Program Goal

The primary goal of the work-based education program is to teach employability skills; gain job- or site-specific skills; foster work-oriented relationships with adults; and acquire the attitudes, skills, and knowledge of life roles in real work settings.

Step 2: Develop Program Objectives

The authors suggest that the reader select appropriate skill areas for his or her students and write instructional objectives to measure results. According to Mager (1984), "These statements are descriptions of intended results of instruction. They are descriptions of the standards we would like students to achieve or surpass" (p. 13). The following school-to-work units list was developed by Bliss (2003) and contains the employability skills necessary for students to successfully enter the modern workforce. The authors encourage the new teacher to review the school-to-work units and develop student objectives.

1. About me/self-awareness: Students explore their interests, skills, abilities, values, learning styles, and occupational preferences through a variety of inventories and activities.

2. Punctuality, attendance, and absenteeism

3. Personal appearance: dress, grooming, and personal cleanliness

4. Good worker character traits: dependability, honesty, positive attitude, willingness to work, and how to deal with boredom at work

5. Communication skills: listening, speaking, reading, writing, nonverbal, body language, sign language, and assertive communication

6. Getting along with supervisors

7. Getting along with coworkers

8. Income taxes and paycheck math

9. Job-seeking skills: preparing a resume, filling out job application forms and other job-related forms, and interviewing for a job

10. Money management

SOURCE: Reprinted with permission from Paula Bliss, M. Ed. Special Education Teacher—www.paulabliss.com.

Step 3: Develop Guide for Program Implementation

The teacher must develop a step-by-step guide for implementing his or her work-based education program. The following steps are recommended for program implementation:

- Meet with local business and secure job training site for the school year.
- Develop all necessary forms for program.
  a. Business partner contract
  b. Parent permission
  c. Student commitment

- Procure all materials needed to successfully implement the program.
- Outline the vocational and employment skills to be addressed during the school year.
  a. Work performance at the job site
  b. Classroom performance on tests, quizzes, daily work, and projects

- Develop program expectations for students.
  a. Dress code
  b. Classroom and job site behavior

Materials or Resources

Form 9.3: Work-Based Student Evaluation

Form 9.4: Student's Critique of Job Site

Resource 9.2: Work Behavior Training Strategies for Vocational Training With Students With Disabilities

Resource 9.3: Job Accommodations for People With Mental Retardation (MR) or Other Developmental Disabilities (DD)

Form 9.1   High School 4-Year Plan

Name: _____   Graduation year: _____

Program of study (check):

_____ College preparatory (CP)

_____ Career technical preparatory (CT)

Area of concentration: _____

(Examples of areas: agriculture, automotive, business, construction, culinary arts, graphic arts, and technology)

_____ Dual seal (both CP and CT)

Total units required for graduation: _____ units

Subject Area[a]	9th Grade	10th Grade	11th Grade	12th Grade
English				
Math				
Science				
Social studies				
Foreign language				
Physical education and health				
Career technical				
Electives				

[a]List specific courses or course numbers in the designated subject area students will take each year.

Dates reviewed: _____

_____

Form 9.2   High School Unit of Credit Checklist

Name: _____   Graduation Year: _____

_____ Total units required for selected program of study

NOTE: A = first semester course; B = second semester course.

English (_____ units required)

☐ 9A   ☐ 10A   ☐ 11A   ☐ 12A   ☐ Other: _____
☐ 9B   ☐ 10B   ☐ 11B   ☐ 12B   ☐ Other: _____

Math (_____ units required)

☐ Algebra 1A   ☐ Geometry A   ☐ Algebra 2A   ☐ Other: _____
☐ Algebra 1B   ☐ Geometry B   ☐ Algebra 2B   ☐ Other: _____
☐ Adv Alg/Trig A   ☐ Algebra 3A   ☐ Calculus A
☐ Adv Alg/Trig B   ☐ Algebra 3B   ☐ Calculus B

Science (_____ units required)

☐ Intro Physics A   ☐ Biology A   ☐ Physics A   ☐ Chemistry A   ☐ Anatomy A
☐ Intro Physics B   ☐ Biology B   ☐ Physics B   ☐ Chemistry B   ☐ Anatomy B
☐ Other: _____
☐ Other: _____

Social studies (_____ units required)

☐ World History A   ☐ American History A   ☐ Citizenship/Civics   ☐ Psychology
☐ World History B   ☐ American History B   ☐ Economics
☐ Sociology   ☐ World Geography   ☐ Other: _____

☐ Physical education (_____ units required)

☐ Health/Safety   ☐ Personal Fitness

☐ Foreign language (_____ units required)

☐ Spanish 1A   ☐ Spanish 2A   ☐ German 1A   ☐ French 1A   ☐ Other: _____
☐ Spanish 1B   ☐ Spanish 2B   ☐ German 1B   ☐ French 1B   ☐ Other: _____

☐ Electives (_____ units required)

(1) _____   (3) _____   (5) _____   (7) _____

(2) _____   (4) _____   (6) _____   (8) _____

☐ Other: _____

Resource 9.1   Students With Disabilities Preparing for Postsecondary Education: Know Your Rights and Responsibilities

- **As a student with a disability leaving high school and entering postsecondary education, will I see differences in my rights and how they are addressed?**

Yes. Section 504 and Title II protect elementary, secondary, and postsecondary students from discrimination. Nevertheless, several of the requirements that apply through high school are different from the requirements that apply beyond high school. For instance, Section 504 requires a school district to provide a free appropriate public education (FAPE) to each child with a disability in the district's jurisdiction. Whatever the disability, a school district must identify an individual's education needs and provide any general or special education and related aids and services necessary to meet those needs as well as it is meeting the needs of students without disabilities.

Unlike your high school, your postsecondary school is not required to provide FAPE. Rather, your postsecondary school is required to provide appropriate academic adjustments as necessary to ensure that it does not discriminate on the basis of disability. In addition, if your postsecondary school provides housing to nondisabled students, it must provide comparable, convenient, and accessible housing to students with disabilities at the same cost.

Other important differences you need to know, even before you arrive at your postsecondary school, are addressed in the remaining questions.

- **May a postsecondary school deny my admission because I have a disability?**

No. If you meet the essential requirements for admission, a postsecondary school may not deny your admission simply because you have a disability.

- **Do I have to inform a postsecondary school that I have a disability?**

No. However, if you want the school to provide an academic adjustment, you must identify yourself as having a disability. Likewise, you should let the school know about your disability if you want to ensure that you are assigned to accessible facilities. In any event, your disclosure of a disability is always voluntary.

- **What academic adjustments must a postsecondary school provide?**

The appropriate academic adjustment must be determined based on your disability and individual needs. Academic adjustments include modifications to academic requirements and auxiliary aids and services, for example, arranging for priority registration; reducing a course load; substituting one course for another; providing note takers, recording devices, sign language interpreters, extended time for testing, and, if telephones are provided in dorm rooms, a TTY in your dorm room; and equipping school computers with screen-reading, voice recognition, or other adaptive software or hardware.

In providing an academic adjustment, your postsecondary school is not required to lower or effect substantial modifications to essential requirements. For example, although your school may be required to provide extended testing time, it is not required to change the substantive content of the test. In addition, your postsecondary school does not have to make modifications that would fundamentally alter the nature of a service, program, or activity or would result in undue financial or administrative burdens. Finally, your postsecondary school does not have to provide personal attendants, individually prescribed devices, readers for personal use or study, or other devices or services of a personal nature, such as tutoring and typing.

- **If I want an academic adjustment, what must I do?**

You must inform the school that you have a disability and need an academic adjustment. Unlike your school district, your postsecondary school is not required to identify you as having a disability or assess your needs.

Your postsecondary school may require you to follow reasonable procedures to request an academic adjustment. You are responsible for knowing and following these procedures. Postsecondary schools usually include, in their publications providing general information, information on the procedures and contacts for requesting an academic adjustment. Such publications include recruitment materials, catalogs, and student handbooks and are often available on school Web sites. Many schools also have staff whose purpose is to assist students with disabilities. If you are unable to locate the procedures, ask a school official, such as an admissions officer or counselor.

- **When should I request an academic adjustment?**

Although you may request an academic adjustment from your postsecondary school at any time, you should request it as early as possible. Some academic adjustments may take more time to provide than others. You should follow your school's procedures to ensure that your school has enough time to review your request and provide an appropriate academic adjustment.

- **Do I have to prove that I have a disability to obtain an academic adjustment?**

Generally, yes. Your school probably will require you to provide documentation that shows you have a current disability and need an academic adjustment.

- **What documentation should I provide?**

Schools may set reasonable standards for documentation. Some schools require more documentation than others. They may require you to provide documentation prepared by an appropriate professional, such as a medical doctor, psychologist, or other qualified diagnostician. The required documentation may include one or more of the following: a diagnosis of your current disability; the date of the diagnosis; how the diagnosis was reached; the credentials of the professional; how your disability affects a major life activity; and how the disability affects your academic performance. The documentation should provide enough information for you and your school to decide what is an appropriate academic adjustment.

Although an Individualized Education Program (IEP) or Section 504 plan, if you have one, may help identify services that have been effective for you, it generally is not sufficient documentation. This is because postsecondary education presents different demands than high school education, and what you need to meet these new demands may be different. Also in some cases, the nature of a disability may change.

If the documentation that you have does not meet the postsecondary school's requirements, a school official must tell you in a timely manner what additional documentation you need to provide. You may need a new evaluation in order to provide the required documentation.

- **Who has to pay for a new evaluation?**

Neither your high school nor your postsecondary school is required to conduct or pay for a new evaluation to document your disability and need for an academic adjustment. This may mean that you have to pay or find funding to pay an appropriate professional to do it. If you are eligible for services through your state vocational

(Continued)

Resource 9.1 (Continued)

rehabilitation agency, you may qualify for an evaluation at no cost to you. You may locate your state vocational rehabilitation agency through this Department of Education Web page: www.ed.gov/parents/needs/speced/resources.html.

- **Once the school has received the necessary documentation from me, what should I expect?**

The school will review your request in light of the essential requirements for the relevant program to help determine an appropriate academic adjustment. It is important to remember that the school is not required to lower or waive essential requirements. If you have requested a specific academic adjustment, the school may offer that academic adjustment or an alternative one if the alternative also would be effective. The school may also conduct its own evaluation of your disability and needs at its own expense.

You should expect your school to work with you in an interactive process to identify an appropriate academic adjustment. Unlike the experience you may have had in high school, however, do not expect your postsecondary school to invite your parents to participate in the process or to develop an IEP for you.

- **What if the academic adjustment we identified is not working?**

Let the school know as soon as you become aware that the results are not what you expected. It may be too late to correct the problem if you wait until the course or activity is completed. You and your school should work together to resolve the problem.

- **May a postsecondary school charge me for providing an academic adjustment?**

No. Furthermore, it may not charge students with disabilities more for participating in its programs or activities than it charges students who do not have disabilities.

- **What can I do if I believe the school is discriminating against me?**

Practically every postsecondary school must have a person—frequently called the Section 504 Coordinator, ADA Coordinator, or Disability Services Coordinator—who coordinates the school's compliance with Section 504 or Title II or both laws. You may contact this person for information about how to address your concerns.

The school also must have grievance procedures. These procedures are not the same as the due process procedures with which you may be familiar from high school. However, the postsecondary school's grievance procedures must include steps to ensure that you may raise your concerns fully and fairly and must provide for the prompt and equitable resolution of complaints.

School publications, such as student handbooks and catalogs, usually describe the steps you must take to start the grievance process. Often, schools have both formal and informal processes. If you decide to use a grievance process, you should be prepared to present all the reasons that support your request.

If you are dissatisfied with the outcome from using the school's grievance procedures or you wish to pursue an alternative to using the grievance procedures, you may file a complaint against the school with OCR or in a court. You may learn more about the OCR complaint process from the brochure How to File a Discrimination Complaint with the Office for Civil Rights, which you may obtain at http://www.ed.gov/ocr/docs/howto.html.

SOURCE: U.S. Department of Education, Office for Civil Rights, *Students with Disabilities Preparing for Postsecondary Education: Know Your Rights and Responsibilities*, Washington, D.C. 20202.

Form 9.3   Work-Based Student Evaluation

Student name: _____   Date: _____

Job site: _____

Task(s): _____

_____

Levels of Performance

Area	Excellent 4 Points	Satisfactory 3 Points	Needs Improvement 2 Points	Unsatisfactory 0 Points	Total
Uses time card					
Demonstrates good hygiene and neat appearance					
Follows directions					
Greets employer appropriately					
Begins work immediately					
Remains on task					
Asks for more work/begins a new task when completed					
Leaves work site appropriately					

Comments:

_____

_____

_____

_____

SOURCE: Adapted with permission from Jeromy Williams, Learning Specialist, Harlem High School.

Form 9.4   Student's Critique of Job Site

Student name: _____   Date: _____

Job site: _____   Job coach: _____

Directions: Please answer the following questions:

1. What did you like about the job site?

   _____

   _____

2. What did you dislike about the job site?

   _____

   _____

3. Do the requirements of this job match your interests?   Yes   or   No

   _____

   _____

4. Do the requirements of this job match your abilities?   Yes   or   No

   _____

   _____

5. Are there any other skills needed to obtain this type of job?   Yes   or   No

   _____

   _____

6. Is this a realistic employment goal for you?   Yes   or   No
   If yes, identify tentative job goal:

   _____

   _____

SOURCE: Adapted with permission from Jeromy Williams, Learning Specialist, Harlem High School.

Resource 9.2   Work Behavior Training Strategies for Vocational Training With Students With Disabilities

1. Start with initial orientation to task, environment, materials, appropriate dress, and expectations: outcomes.

2. Design training sessions for success. Prior to beginning a work session, discuss what will be done and what the reinforcement will be. The reinforcement needs to be tangible and accessible.

3. Identify expected behaviors (vocational and social) to maximize efficient use of time allotted to do task. This should be reviewed frequently. This should be reinforced on the job whenever possible.

4. Be sure to set goals that the student will be able to reach (accessible) and the reinforcement is immediate (tangible) and it is something that motivates the student.

5. Once behavioral obstacles are identified, develop behavior plan to ensure consistency among staff in addressing these behaviors.

6. Use verbal agreements or contracts when setting up what the task and reinforcement will be. Use verbal and visual reminders during the task if the student is getting distracted, tired, or losing motivation to complete the work agreement. For example: After working for 1 hour, we will take a coffee break, take a walk to get the mail, rest, or fill out your time sheet so you get paid for the work done.

7. Prior to the start of each task, based on task analysis, demonstrate appropriate operation/execution of task in slow graduated steps (well thought out). During training, take nothing for granted, no matter how simple the task may appear (backward chaining).

8. Teach one task at a time. Backward chaining: Complete a task sequence with the student, and have him or her be responsible for the last piece in the task. During this time, the staff person is doing the other parts of the task and explaining the task, "getting the whole picture." Once the student has mastered a step, add the next step and so on until the student is doing all steps of the task.

9. Through observation, make note of any physical, cognitive, and social deficits, and be ready to adapt the job or develop compensatory strategies or both.

10. Use written or picture task cards to help with memory and sequencing of the task procedure. Possibly, have a check-off sheet that the student can use to check off each step as it has been completed. This gives the student a visual guide to see his or her progress and how close he or she is to completing the task (helps deal with fatigue).

11. Develop weekly schedules to be distributed to and discussed with students.

12. Use a ratio of one teacher or trainer to two students (1:1 even better).

13. Be extremely sensitive to safety issues (i.e., allergies, medications, physical sensitivities and limitations, etc.).

(Continued)

Resource 9.2 (Continued)

14. Always be certain (1) that necessary materials and equipment are available at the beginning of the work period and (2) that students, with assistance when necessary, put all materials back in appropriate storage area.

15. Use common sense when assigning job sites.

16. As a trainer, it is essential that you are well organized and fully understand expected outcomes.

17. Try to treat students as workers, not children.

18. Data collection is very important.

19. Try not to intervene immediately, using common sense. Allow the student some time to either work out the problem or ask for assistance.

20. Comments made daily should be concise and relative to weaker areas. Be specific, not general. From these comments, goals and objectives will emerge and subsequently tighten up your training program. Again, do not assign too many tasks.

21. Be consistent with developing organizational and teaching strategies; student learning will be enhanced.

22. When teaching a task, keep it specific and simple, demonstrate, monitor, and then intervene.

23. Practice and repetition of activities, as well as feedback on performance, will strengthen the student's confidence to do the job.

24. Most important, focus on behavior in a new environment coupled with new expectations—you may discover different aspects or behaviors or both relative to students.

25. Focus primarily, where necessary, on behavior. Vocational skills will emerge as behaviors are controlled.

26. Each day should start with a review of training. If appropriate, follow-up discussion is very helpful.

27. When you are instructing, always ask questions, particularly during orientation to the job.

28. Very important: As you observe students working, try to determine the need for use of occupational therapy, physical therapy, speech, and so on.

SOURCE: Reprinted with permission from Paula Bliss, M. Ed. Special Education Teacher—www.paulabliss.com.

Resource 9.3   Job Accommodations for People With Mental Retardation (MR) or
Other Developmental Disabilities (DD)

Cognitive Limitations

Reading

- Provide pictures, symbols, or diagrams instead of words.
- Read written information to employee or provide written information on audiotape.
- Use voice output on computer.
- Use Reading Pen on single words.
- Use line guide to identify or highlight one line of text at a time.

Writing

- Provide templates or forms to prompt information requested.
- Allow verbal response instead of written response.
- Allow typed response instead of written response.
- Use voice input and spell-check on computer.
- Use a scribe to write the employee's response.
- Provide ample space on forms requiring written response.
- Use voice-activated recorder to record verbal instructions.

Calculations

- Allow use of large-display or talking calculator and use counter or ticker.
- Make precounted or premeasured poster or jig.
- Provide talking tape measure and liquid level indicators.
- Mark the measuring cup with a "fill to here" line.

Organization

- Minimize clutter and color code items or resources.
- Provide A-B-C and 1-2-3 chart.
- Divide large tasks into multiple smaller tasks.
- Use symbols instead of words, and use print labels instead of handwritten labels.

Time Management

- Provide verbal prompts (reminders).
- Provide written or symbolic reminders.
- Use alarm watch or beeper.
- Use jig for assembly to increase productivity.
- Arrange materials in order of use.
- Use task list with numbers or symbols.
- Avoid isolated workstations.
- Provide space for job coach.
- Provide additional training or retraining as needed.

(Continued)

Resource 9.3 (Continued)

Gross and Fine Motor Limitations

Computer Use

- Use keyguard.
- Use alternative input devices, such as speech recognition, trackball, and joystick.

Telephone Use

- Use large-button phone.
- Use phone with universal symbols (fire, police, and doctor).
- Use phone with speed dial, clearly labeled.
- Use receiver holder.
- Use headset.

Workstation Use

- Place antifatigue mats at workstation.
- Use motorized scooter.
- Use stools at workstations.
- Move items within reach.
- Provide frequent rest breaks.

Tool Use

- Use ergonomic tools, handle build-ups, or other tool adaptations.
- Use orthopedic writing aids.
- Use grip aids.
- Use jig or brace.

Social Interaction

- Implement a structure of positive feedback.
- Use visual performance charts.
- Provide tangible rewards.
- Use coworkers as mentors, and provide sensitivity training (disability awareness) to all employees.
- Use Employee Assistance Program (EAP).
- Provide job coach, and use training videos to demonstrate appropriate behavior in workplace.
- Model appropriate social skills, such as where to eat, when to hug, how to pay for coffee, and how to ask for help.

SOURCE: Reprinted with permission of the Job Accommodation Network, a service of the U.S. Department of Education Office of Disability Employment Policy.

10 Professional Development for the Special Education Teacher

Man's mind, stretched by a new idea, never goes back to its original dimensions.

—Oliver Wendell Holmes

Professional development is typically defined in the field of education as any course of action taken by a school employee for the purpose of increasing his or her skills in a particular academic area or knowledge of a specific educational topic. School systems often develop professional development programs that are global by design and primarily focus on identified or perceived needs of the entire system; often, however, these programs do not necessarily address the individual needs of teachers and staff. The landscape of special education is in a constant state of change, and the new teacher must assume the personal responsibility of devising an individual plan that is continuous by design and will enable him or her to survive and thrive in the profession during this wake of change. The development of a solid plan is essential for both new and veteran teachers to keep abreast of new instructional techniques, strategies, and programs that impact student learning and achievement; to acquire knowledge of current trends in special and regular education; and to obtain information pertaining to new legal developments in the profession that could impact students and programs. Stephen Covey's "Habit 7: Sharpen the Saw" accurately depicts the need for the first-year special education teacher to devise a personal, ongoing, professional development program. Covey (1992) states, "If you don't improve and renew yourself constantly, you'll fall into entropy, closed systems and styles. At one end of the continuum is entropy (everything breaks down), and at the other end is continuous improvement, innovation, and refinement" (p. 47). In a time when the education profession as a whole is being held under a high-powered microscope, special education teachers throughout the country are finding their programs and services being scrutinized for productivity and effectiveness. Teachers who constantly "sharpen the saw" will find themselves to be on the cutting edge of the profession and in a constant state of professional and personal growth. In this chapter, five strategies are presented that will assist the beginning teacher in his or her professional development journey.

STRATEGY 1: FORMULATE A PROFESSIONAL DEVELOPMENT PLAN

The authors recommend that the special education teacher begin developing a professional development plan prior to the beginning of each new school year. The plan should include short- and long-term professional goals and a timeline for goal completion, and note the teacher's particular areas of interest. The plan should also include any staff development or training needed to effectively perform his or her current job or contribute to his or her school's current education initiatives. A completed professional development plan can assist the new teacher in performing a self-assessment at the end of each school year and serve as a record of professional pursuits and activities over a period of time. The plan should be placed in the teacher's portfolio (see Strategy 2) at the end of each school year.

Materials or Resources

Form 10.1: Professional Development Plan

STRATEGY 2: DEVELOP A PROFESSIONAL PORTFOLIO

The development of a professional portfolio is essential for all educators who are seeking employment or documenting personal growth in the field. The portfolio is a tool that teachers can use to showcase personal attributes, skills, and activities; it serves to highlight one's accomplishments as a professional educator. Electronic portfolios are becoming more popular than traditional hard copy due to the convenience of the Internet and the ease with which Web page portfolios can be modified and updated. The authors recommend that the reader update and review the portfolio on a regular basis and reflect on the artifacts that one has collected throughout his or her journey.

Materials or Resources

Form 10.2: Portfolio Format for the Professional Educator

STRATEGY 3: JOIN A PROFESSIONAL ORGANIZATION

The authors suggest that the new special education teacher join at least one professional education organization. Often, these organizations distribute valuable information to their members through magazines, newsletters, journals, Web sites, or all these; provide members with liability coverage; provide the new teacher with networking opportunities; and conduct annual conferences at the state or national level. The authors strongly recommend that new teachers attend at least one professional conference a year. Professional conferences for educators typically follow a general format that includes at least one general session with a keynote speaker, a variety of small-group sessions on specific topics, and numerous how-to workshops that engage participants in interactive learning activities. The authors suggest that teachers review all conference information in advance and plan a daily agenda that will maximize their conference experience. Conference brochures can often be obtained in advance by visiting the sponsoring organization's Web site. Conferences can be viewed as one-stop resource centers that provide numerous opportunities to exchange ideas, materials, and resources with other special education teachers and possibly obtain staff development or continuing education credit. Staff development credit can be used for recertification in some states. The authors have created a form designed to be used as a planning guide to ensure that one maximizes his or her opportunities and time at any conference. A list of professional organizations is provided in Resource 10.1. The authors have included a list of additional organizations that can provide the beginning special education teacher with resource information pertaining to specific diseases or health conditions.

Materials or Resources

Form 10.3: Conference Planning Guide

Resource 10.1: The Special Education Teacher's Guide to Professional Organizations

STRATEGY 4: READ PROFESSIONAL JOURNALS AND BOOKS

The reading of educational journals and books on a regular basis is necessary to stay current in the profession. The media centers of most schools have educational journals and books available for staff members. If the new teacher finds his or her school's media center lacking in a particular area, however, he or she should check with the head librarian to determine if additional resources can be ordered. The Internet is a valuable tool to locate and purchase current books and other resource material. Some of the larger bookstore chains carry extensive inventories online and provide speedy delivery of purchases. The authors suggest summarizing all material that the reader has found to be of particular interest and maintaining the information in a three-ring notebook, which is organized by subject areas or topics and allows for quick referencing or reviewing by the reader. A listing of current periodicals and books pertaining to special and regular education can be found in Resources 10.2 and 10.3.

Materials or Resources

Resource 10.2: The Special Education Teacher's Guide to Professional Periodicals

Resource 10.3: The Special Education Teacher's Guide to Professional Books

Resource 10.4: Web Sites for Special Education Teachers

STRATEGY 5: ENROLL IN ADVANCED COLLEGE COURSES OR STAFF DEVELOPMENT CLASSES

The authors suggest that the new teacher enroll in advanced college courses or local staff development classes offered through the school system once a comfort level has been reached in his or her current teaching position. Often, new college graduates are eager to "have it all" and misjudge the amount of personal energy required for a new teaching job and pursuing a graduate degree. The authors recommend that the new teacher wait approximately 3 years before pursuing a new degree or adding an additional area of certification. Finally, the authors remind the reader that college courses are usually more expensive; staff development classes, however, are offered at a low or no cost to school employees, scheduled after school hours or during the summer, and give credit toward recertification.

Form 10.1   Professional Development Plan

School year: _____

Special education teacher: _____

Certification number: _____   Expiration date: _____

Licensure number: _____   Expiration date: _____

Certification area/grade level (list):

_____

Short-Range Professional Goals (Completion Within 1 Year):

Professional Goals	Completion Date
1.	
2.	
3.	
4.	
5.	

Long-Range Professional Goals (Completion Within 5 Years):

Professional Goals	Completion Date
1.	
2.	
3.	
4.	
5.	

Form 10.2   Portfolio Format for the Professional Educator

Portfolio Contents Checklist:

_____ Cover page

_____ Table of contents

_____ Personal resume

_____ Philosophy of education

_____ Graduate coursework

_____ Practicum and student teaching experiences

_____ Descriptions of special projects or programs

_____ Technology applications and skills

_____ Professional development activities

_____ Copy of awards or certificates

_____ Copy of certification and/or licensures

_____ Copy of letters of recommendation

Portfolio Tips:

A special education teacher's professional portfolio should

1. Be placed in a three-ring notebook with dividers and/or tabs

2. Be neat, clean, well organized, and have a consistent appearance

3. Contain only copies of important documents in case an interviewer wants to keep it

4. Contain current information, just like a resume

Form 10.3   Conference Planning Guide

Conference name: _____

Conference dates: _____

Conference location: _____

Sponsoring organization: _____

Conference cost: $_____

1. Registration fee: $_____

2. Hotel accommodations: $_____

3. Travel/mileage: $_____

   TOTAL EXPENSE: $_____

Conference theme or objectives:

1. _____

2. _____

3. _____

4. _____

5. _____

Personal Conference Schedule

Date	Time	Session Title	Location

Resource 10.1   The Special Education Teacher's Guide to Professional Organizations

American Association on Mental Retardation
444 N. Capitol Street NW, Suite 846
Washington, DC 20001
Telephone: 202-387-1968
Toll free: 800-424-3688
Web site: www.aamr.org

American Council of the Blind
1155 15th Street, Suite 720
Washington, DC 20005
Telephone: 202-467-5081
Toll free: 800-424-8666
Web site: www.acb.org

American Federation of Teachers (AFT)
555 New Jersey Avenue NW, 10th Floor
Washington, DC 20001
Telephone: 202-879-4400

American Juvenile Arthritis Organization
1330 W. Peachtree Street
Atlanta, GA 30309
Telephone: 404-872-7100
Toll free: 800-283-7800
Web site: www.arthritis.org/ajao

American Speech-Language-Hearing Association
10801 Rockville Pike
Rockville, MD 20852
Telephone: 301-897-5700
Toll free: 800-638-8255
Web site: www.asha.org

ARC of the United States
500 E. Border Street, #300
Arlington, TX 76010
Telephone: 817-261-6003
e-mail: info@thearc.org
Web site: www.thearc.org

Association for Persons in Supported Employment
1627 Monument Avenue, Suite 301
Richmond, VA 23220
Telephone: 804-278-9187
Fax: 804-278-9377
e-mail: tamara@apse.org
Web site: www.apse.org

Autism Society of America
7910 Woodmount Avenue, Suite 650

Bethesda, MD 20814
Telephone: 301-657-0881
Toll free: 800-3AUTISM
Web site: www.autism-society.org

Council for Children with Behavioral
Disorders (CCBD)
c/o The Council for Exceptional Children
1920 Association Drive
Reston, VA 20192-1589
William Evans, President
Telephone: 703-620-3660
Fax: 703-264-9494

Council for Exceptional Children (CEC)
1920 Association Drive
Reston, VA 22091-1587
Nancy D. Safer, Contact
Telephone: 703-620-3660 or 703-264-9462
Fax: 703-264-9494

Division for Early Childhood (DEC)
Council for Exceptional Children
1920 Association Drive
Reston, VA 20191-1589
Tess Bennett, President
Telephone: 703-620-3660
Fax: 703-264-9494

Division for Learning Disabilities
c/o Council for Exceptional Children
1920 Association Drive
Reston, VA 20191-1589
Web site: www.dldcec.org

Division on Career Development
and Transition (DCDT)
c/o The Council for Exceptional Children
1920 Association Drive
Reston, VA 20191
Robert Miller, President
Telephone: 703-620-3660
Fax: 703-264-9494

Division on Visual Impairment (DVI)
c/o Council for Exceptional Children
1920 Association Drive
Reston, VA 20191-1589
Roseanna Davidson, President
Telephone: 703-620-3660
Fax: 703-264-9494

Foundation for Exceptional Children (FEC)
1920 Association Drive
Reston, VA 20191
Ken Collins, Executive Director
Telephone: 703-620-1054
Fax: 703-264-9494

Learning Disabilities Association of America
4156 Library Road
Pittsburgh, PA 15234
Telephone: 412-341-1515
Toll free: 888-300-6710

Muscular Dystrophy Association of America
3300 E. Sunrise Drive
Tucson, AZ 85718
Telephone: 800-572-1717
Web site: www.mdausa.org

National Alliance of Black School
Educators (NABSE)
2816 Georgia Avenue NW
Washington, DC 20001
Quentin Lawson, Executive Director
Telephone: 202-483-1549
Fax: 202-483-8323

National Association of
Developmental Disabilities Council
1234 Massachusetts Avenue NW, Suite 103
Washington, DC 20005
Telephone: 202-347-1234
Fax: 202-347-4023
e-mail: mgray@naddc.org
Web site: www.igc.apc.org/NADDC

National Association of Early Childhood Teacher
Educators (NAECTE)
c/o Dr. Jean Isenberg
9671 Mason Bluff Ct.
Burke, VA 22015-3148

Dr. Jean Isenberg, President
Telephone: 703-993-2037
Fax: 703-993-2013

National Association of Professional
Educators (NAPE)
412 1st Street SE
Washington, DC 20003
Philip Strittmatter, Executive Secretary
Telephone: 202-484-8969
Fax: 202-863-9361

National Down Syndrome Society
666 Broadway, 8th Floor
New York, NY 10012-2317
Telephone: 212-460-9330
Toll free: 800-221-4602
e-mail: info@ndss.org
Web site: www.ndss.org

National Education Association (NEA)
1201 16th Street NW
Washington, DC 20036
Telephone: 202-833-4000

Spina Bifida Association of America
4590 MacArthur Blvd. NW, Suite 250
Washington, DC 20007
Telephone: 202-944-3285
Toll free: 800-621-3141
Web site: www.sbaa.org

United Cerebral Palsy
1660 L Street NW, Suite 700
Washington, DC 20036-5602
Telephone: 202-776-0406
Toll free: 800-872-5827
Fax: 202-776-0414
e-mail: webmaster@ucp.org
Web site: www.ucpa.org

Resource 10.2   The Special Education Teacher's Guide to Professional Periodicals

- *Autism Aspergers Digest*

- *Behavioral Disorders*

- *Education and Training in Mental Retardation*

- *Exceptional Child Education Resources*

- *Exceptional Children*

- *Exceptional Parent*

- *Focus on Exceptional Children*

- *Journal of Learning Disabilities*

- *Journal of Special Education*

- *Journal of Speech and Hearing Services in the Schools*

- *Journal of Visual Impairment & Blindness*

- *Learning Disability Quarterly*

- *Phi Delta Kappan*

- *Preventing School Failure*

- *Remedial and Special Education*

- *Teaching Exceptional Children*

Resource 10.3   The Special Education Teacher's Guide to Professional Books

Adapting Curriculum & Instruction for
Special Needs Students
Author: June Bigge
Publisher: Brooks/Cole
Date: February 1999

Asperger Syndrome: A Practical Guide for Teachers
Author: Val Cumine
Publisher: Taylor & Francis
Date: April 1998

Assessing Special Needs Students
Author: Libby Cohen
Publisher: Addison Wesley Longman
Date: January 1998

Assessing Students With Special Needs
Authors: James A. McLoughlin et al.
Publisher: Prentice Hall PTR
Date: March 2004

Best Teaching Practices for Reaching
All Learners
Author: Randi Stone
Publisher: Corwin Press
Date: March 2004

Building Classroom Discipline
Author: C. M. Charles
Publisher: Allyn & Bacon
Date: April 2004

Children Don't Come With an Instruction Manual:
A Teacher's Guide to Problems That Affect Learners
Author: Wendy Moss
Publisher: Teachers College Press
Date: April 2004

The Classroom of Choice: Giving Students
What They Need and Getting What You Want
Author: Jonathan C. Erwin
Publisher: Association for Supervision &
Curriculum Development
Date: May 2004

Collaboration: A Success Strategy for Special Educators
Author: Sharon F. Cramer
Publisher: Allyn & Bacon
Date: 1998

Collaborative Elementary Teaching: A Casebook for
Elementary Special & General Educators
Author: Kathleen C. Harris
Publisher: PRO-ED
Date: February 1998

Collaborative Secondary Teaching: A Casebook for
Secondary & Special Educators
Authors: Kathleen Harris and Marcia Smith
Publisher: PRO-ED
Date: February 1998

Complete IEP Guide: How to Advocate
for Your Special Education Child
Author: Lawrence Siegel
Publisher: Nolo Press
Date: January 1998

Concise Encyclopedia of Special Education: A Reference
for the Education of the Handicapped and Other
Exceptional Children and Adults
Authors: Cecil R. Reynolds et al.
Publisher: John Wiley
Date: March 2004

Conducting Individualized Education Program
Meetings That Withstand Due Process: The Informal
Evidentiary Proceeding
Author: James N. Hollis
Publisher: Charles C Thomas
Date: April 1998

Cooperative Learning & Strategies for Inclusions:
Celebrating Diversity in the Classroom
Author: Joanne Putnam
Publisher: Brookes
Date: June 1998

Creating Inclusive Classrooms:
Effective and Reflective Practices
Author: Spencer J. Salend
Publisher: Prentice Hall PTR
Date: May 2004

Exceptional Lives: Special Education
in Today's Schools
Author: Ann P. Turnbull
Publisher: Prentice Hall
Date: July 1998

(Continued)

Resource 10.3 (Continued)

Finding Help When Your Child Is Struggling in School
Author: Lawrence Greene
Publisher: Golden Books Adult Publishing Group
Date: September 1998

Florida Teacher Certification Exam Emotionally Handicapped
Author: Kathy Schnirman
Publisher: A S A P Abstracts
Date: January 1998

Fundamentals of Special Education: What Every Teacher Needs to Know
Authors: Richard Culatta and James Tompkins
Publisher: Macmillan Library
Date: August 1998

The General Educator's Guide to Special Education: A Resource Handbook for All Who Teach Students With Special Needs
Author: Jody L. Maanum
Publisher: Peytral
Date: January 2004

Handbook for Pre-school SEN Provision: The Code of Practice in Relation to the Early Years
Author: Chris Spencer
Publisher: Taylor & Francis
Date: April 1998

Including Families of Children With Special Needs: A How-to-Do-It
Authors: Sandra Feinberg, Kathleen Deerr, Barbara Jordan, and Michelle Langa
Publisher: Neal-Schuman
Date: December 1998

Including Students With Special Needs: A Practical Guide for Classroom Teachers
Authors: Marilyn Friend and William Bursuck
Publisher: Allyn & Bacon
Date: June 1998

Introduction to Special Education: Teaching in an Age of Challenge
Author: Deborah Smith
Publisher: Allyn & Bacon
Date: 1998

Just Kids: Visiting a Class for Children With Special Needs
Author: Ellen Senisi
Publisher: Dutton Children's Book
Date: February 1998

Managing the Adolescent Classroom: Lessons From Outstanding Teachers
Author: Glenda Beamon Crawford
Publisher: Corwin Press
Date: May 2004

One-Minute Discipline: Classroom Management Strategies That Work
Author: Arnie Bianco
Publisher: John Wiley
Date: October 2002

The Power of Imagery: Watch Learning Problems Disappear
Author: Mildred Gifford
Publisher: GiffOdess Books
Date: January 1998

PRAXIS II Subject Area Assessment Emotionally Handicapped
Author: Kathy Schnirmnan
Publisher: A S A P Abstracts
Date: January 1998

PRAXIS II Subject Area Assessment Special Education
Author: Roberta Ramsey
Publisher: A S A P Abstracts
Date: January 1998

Promising Practices Connecting Schools to Families of Children With Special Needs
Author: Diana B. Hiatt-Michael
Publisher: Information Age
Date: January 2004

Reading for Meaning: An Illustrated Alternative Approach to Reading
Author: Jon Eisenson
Publisher: PRO-ED
Date: July 1998

*Special Educational Needs: A Resource
for Practitioners*
Author: Michael Farrell
Publisher: Corwin Press
Date: February 2004

Special Educational Needs in the Early Years
Author: Ruth A. Wilson
Publisher: Routledge
Date: June 1998

*Special Education's Failed System:
A Question of Eligibility*
Author: Joel Macht
Publisher: Greenwood
Date: September 1998

*The Special-Needs Reading List:
An Annotated Guide to the Best
Publications for Parents & Professionals*
Author: Wilma K. Sweeney
Publisher: Woodbine House
Date: January 1998

*Teaching Students With Special Needs in
Inclusive Settings*
Authors: Tom E. Smith, Edward Polloway, James
Patton, and Carol Dowdy
Publisher: Allyn & Bacon
Date: 1998

*Teaching Study Skills & Strategies to Students
Who Are LD, ADD & At-Risk*
Authors: Stephen Strichart, Charles Mangrum, and
Patricia Iannuzzi
Publisher: Allyn & Bacon
Date: April 1998

*Technology and the Diverse Learner: A Guide to
Classroom Practice*
Authors: Marty Bray et al.
Publisher: Corwin Press
Date: May 2004

Theorizing Special Education
Authors: Catherine Clark, Alan Dyson, and Alan
Millward
Publisher: Routledge
Date: June 1998

*Very Young Children With Special Needs: A Formative
Approach for the Twenty-First Century*
Authors: Vikki F. Howard et al.
Publisher: Merrill College
Date: February 2004

*Vocational and Transition Services for Adolescents
With Emotional and Behavioral Disorders:
Strategies and Best Practices*
Authors: Michael Bullis et al.
Publisher: Research Press
Date: January 2004

*What Every Teacher Should Know About Classroom
Management and Discipline*
Author: Donna E. Walker Tileston
Publisher: Corwin Press
Date: October 2003

*What Reading Research Tells Us About Children
With Diverse Learning Needs: Bases & Basics*
Authors: Deborah C. Simmons and E. J. Kameenui
Publisher: Lawrence Erlbaum
Date: June 1998

Writing Time: Writing Strategies That Achieve Results
Author: Harriet Jean Azemove
Publisher: Harriet Jean Azemove
Date: January 1998

*Young Children With Special Needs:
A Developmentally Appropriate Approach.
Instructor's Manual & Test Bank*
Authors: Michael D. Davis, Jennifer L. Kilgo, and
Michael Gamel-McCormick
Publisher: Allyn & Bacon
Date: 1998

Resource 10.4   Web Sites for Special Education Teachers

All Kids Grieve www.allkidsgrieve.org	*Federal No Child Left Behind Act of 2001* www.ed.gov/nclb/landing.jhtml#
American Association on Mental Retardation www.aamr.org	*Learning Disabilities Association of America* www.ldanatl.org
American Speech-Language-Hearing Association www.asha.org/default.htm	*Middle School Students and School Life* www.middleweb.com/ContntsStudn.html
Army Deployment Handbook: Resource for Helping Students With War Anxieties www.wood.army.mil/mwr/deploymenthndbook.htm	*National Board for Professional Teaching Standards* www.nbpts.org
Ask ERIC www.ericir.sys.edu	*National Education Association Crisis Communications and Toolkit* www.nea.org/crisis
Association for Supervision and Curriculum Development (ASCD) www.ascd.org	*National Educational Service* www.nes.org
Autism Society of America www.autism-society.org/site/PageServer	*National Transition Alliance for Youth with Disabilities* www.kctcs.net/edp/services/nta.html
CHADD www.chadd.org/research.cfm?cat_id=11	*Quick Training Aid: School-Based Crisis Intervention* www.smhp.psych.ucla.edu/qf/crisis_qt
Council for Exceptional Children www.cec.sped.org	*Safeguarding Your Children at School: Helping Children Deal with a School Bully* www.pta.org/programs/sycsch.htm
Council of Administrators of Special Education www.casecec.org	
Division for Learning Disabilities www.dldcec.org	*U.S. Department of Education* www.ed.gov/offices/OERI/ECI

Resource A

Medical Emergencies in the School Setting

The majority of new special education teachers will enter into their first teaching positions with the skills necessary to meet the academic needs of their students; there is a spectrum of noneducational situations, however, that will typically occur and require the new teacher to react immediately and with extreme decisiveness. The most common of these situations is when a student becomes ill or injured during the school day. The classroom teacher is usually the first adult to respond to injured or ill students and must be able to assess their physical condition at the scene and determine the proper course of action without hesitation.

Resource A includes a comprehensive list and description of common medical situations or emergencies that the authors have found to occur most frequently in the school environment and the appropriate first aid response by the teacher. In addition, a recommended list of first aid supplies for the classroom is provided. All medical information was obtained from the National Safety Council's *First Aid and CPR* (1992). The authors recommend that the new teacher take the following actions before the new school year begins:

• Review the school system's policies and procedures that specifically address how teachers are to handle medical emergencies in the school environment.

• Request updated medical information from parents at the beginning of each school year. A medical history form (Form A.1) has been included. The teacher should review the form and note all significant medical problems.

• The teacher should develop an emergency medical plan for all students who have a significant medical problem or condition (e.g., seizures, allergic to bee stings, and asthma) (Form A.2). A copy of the plan should be kept in the school's main office.

• The teacher should complete a report after each medical incident (Form A.3).

- The teacher should inform all school personnel who will have a significant amount of contact with the student of his or her medical condition or problem (e.g., inform the physical education teacher if the student has asthma).

- The teacher must remember to keep a log of all medical incidents that occur during the school year (Form A.4). These forms need to be kept in a secure location that is easily accessible for teacher or paraprofessional reference.

SECTION 1: COMMON INJURIES AND ILLNESSES

The following are some of the most common injuries and illnesses that the beginning teacher is likely to encounter in the classroom as well as a brief overview of the best course of treatment:

Abrasion

- **Definition:** An injury consisting of the loss of a partial thickness of skin from rubbing or scraping on a hard, rough surface; also called a brush burn, or friction burn (p. 268).
- **Treatment/response:**
  1. Remove all debris.
  2. Wash away from wound with soap and water (p. 68).

Allergic Reaction

- **Definition:** A local or general reaction to an allergen, usually characterized by hives or tissue swelling or dyspnea (p. 268).
- **Treatment/response:**
  1. Seek medical attention.
  2. Call parents.

Asthma

- **Definition:** A condition marked by recurrent attacks of dyspnea with wheezing, due to spasmodic constriction of the bronchi, often as a response to allergens, or to mucous plugs in the bronchioles (p. 269).
- **Treatment/response (p. 195):**
  1. Comfort and reassure victim because emotional stress can make the condition worse.
  2. Many asthmatics carry tablets or inhalers that relax bronchial spasms. Help them in using these medicines.
  3. Help the victim into a comfortable breathing position that he or she chooses. The best position is usually sitting upright.
  4. Place the victim in a room that is as free as possible of common offenders (e.g., dust, feathers, and animals). It should also be free of odors (e.g., tobacco smoke and paint).
  5. Keep conversations with asthmatics brief because they are struggling to breathe.
  6. Increase the drinking of water if possible.

7. Seek medical attention for the following:
   a. Severe, prolonged asthma attacks
   b. Reactions happening after an insect sting or contact with another source that produces an allergic reaction, which could progress to anaphylactic shock
   c. Failure to improve with medication
   d. Breathing that can barely be heard
   e. Increasing bluish skin color
   f. Pulse rate of more than 120 beats per minute

Diabetes Mellitus

- **Definition:** A systemic disease marked by lack of production of insulin, which causes an inability to metabolize carbohydrates, resulting in an increase in blood sugar (p. 271).

Low Blood Sugar Symptoms

Sudden onset

Staggering, poor coordination

Anger, bad temper

Pale color

Confusion, disorientation

Sudden hunger

Sweating

Eventual stupor or unconsciousness

- **Treatment/response:**
  1. Provide sugar!
  2. If the person can swallow without choking, offer any food or drink containing sugar, such as soft drinks, fruit juice, or candy. Do not use diet drinks when blood sugar is low.
  3. If the person does not respond in 10 to 15 minutes, take him or her to the hospital (p. 193).

High Blood Sugar Symptoms

Gradual Onset

Drowsiness

Extreme thirst

Very frequent urination

Flushed skin

Vomiting

Fruity or wine-like breath odor

Heavy breathing

Eventual stupor or unconsciousness

- **Action to take:**
  1. Take the person to the hospital.
  2. If you are uncertain whether the person is suffering from high or low blood sugar, give some sugar-containing food or drink. If there is no response in 10 to 15 minutes, the person needs immediate medical attention.

Heat Cramps

- **Definition:** A painful muscle cramp resulting from excessive loss of salt and water through sweating (p. 272).
- **Treatment/response:**
  1. Move the victim to a cool place.
  2. Rest the cramping muscle.
  3. Give victim a lot of cold water.
  4. Do not massage because it rarely provides relief and may even worsen the pain (p. 162).

Heat Exhaustion

- **Definition:** A prostration caused by excessive loss of water and salt through sweating; characterized by clammy skin and a weak, rapid pulse (p. 272).
- **Treatment/response:**
  1. Move the victim to a cool place.
  2. Keep victim lying down with straight legs elevated 8 to 12 inches.
  3. Cool the victim by applying cold packs or wet towels or cloths. Fan the victim.
  4. Give the victim cold water if he or she is fully conscious.
  5. If no improvement is noted within 30 minutes, seek medical attention (p. 162).

Human Bites

- **Treatment/response:**
  1. Thoroughly wash the wound with soap and water.
  2. Apply a dry, sterile dressing, and seek medical attention (p. 75).

Nosebleed

- **Treatment/response:**

Note: The authors have included only the first three of the steps recommended by the National Safety Council (p. 85).

1. Reassure and keep the victim quiet. Although a large amount of blood may appear to have been lost, most nosebleeds are not serious.
2. Keep the victim in a sitting position to reduce blood pressure.
3. Keep the victim's head tilted slightly forward so that the blood can run out the front of the nose, not down the back of the throat, which causes either choking or nausea and vomiting. (The vomit could be inhaled into the lungs.)
4. Accompany the student to the office or school nurse as soon as possible for further assistance.

Seizure

- **Definition:** A sudden attack or recurrence of a disease; a convulsion; an attack of epilepsy (p. 275).

1. *Generalized tonic-clonic* (also called grand mal): Sudden cry, fall, rigidity, followed by muscle jerks, shallow breathing or temporarily suspended breathing, bluish skin, possible loss of bladder or bowel control, usually lasts a couple of minutes. Normal breathing then starts again. There may be some confusion or fatigue or both, followed by return to full consciousness (p. 193).

   A. *What to do:* Look for medical identification. Protect from nearby hazards. Loosen tie or shirt collars. Protect head from injury. Turn on side to keep airway clear. Reassure when consciousness returns. If single seizure lasted less than 5 minutes, ask if hospital evaluation is wanted. If there are multiple seizures, or if one seizure lasted longer than 5 minutes, call an ambulance. If the person is pregnant, injured, or diabetic, call for aid at once.

   B. *What not to do:* Do not put any hard implement in the mouth. Do not try to hold tongue: It cannot be swallowed. Do not try to give liquids during or just after seizure. Do not use artificial respiration unless breathing is absent after muscle jerks subside or unless water has been inhaled. Do not restrain.

2. *Absence* (also called petit mal): A blank stare, lasting only a few seconds, most common in children. May be accompanied by rapid blinking and some chewing movements of the mouth. The child is unaware of what is going on during the seizure but quickly returns to full awareness once it has stopped. It may result in learning difficulties if not recognized and treated (p. 193).

   A. *What to do:* No first aid is necessary, but if this is the first observation of the seizure(s), medical evaluation should be recommended (p. 193).

SECTION 2: FIRST AID SUPPLIES

The authors recommend the following medical supplies for the classroom's first aid kit:

- Adhesive strip bandages, assorted sizes
- Adhesive tape, 1- and 2-inch rolls
- Antibiotic skin ointment
- Chemical ice pack
- Cotton balls
- Disposable latex gloves
- Elastic bandages, 2-, 3-, and 4-inch width
- Gauze pads, 2×2 and 4×4
- Hydrogen peroxide
- Nonadhering dressing
- Scissors
- Tweezers
- Hand cleaner
- Antiseptic wipes
- Cotton swabs

Form A.1   Medical History

School year: _____

Student name: _____ Date of birth: _____

Grade: _____

Home telephone number: _____

Mother/guardian's work telephone number: _____

e-mail address: _____

Beeper number: _____

Father/guardian's work telephone number: _____

e-mail address: _____

Beeper number: _____

Emergency contact: _____

Name   Relationship   Telephone number

Student's medical problem (please be specific):

_____

_____

_____

_____

_____

Current medication (dosage and time of administration):

_____

_____

_____

Allergies:

_____

_____

Parent/guardian signature: _____ Date: _____

Form A.2   Emergency Medical Plan

School year: _____

Student name: _____   Date of birth: _____

Grade: _____

Medical problem or condition:

_____

_____

_____

_____

_____

_____

_____

Emergency plan of action:

_____

_____

_____

_____

_____

_____

_____

_____

Parent/guardian signature: _____

Teacher signature: _____

School administrator signature: _____

Copy on file in main school office: Yes   or   No

Form A.3   Medical Incident Report

Date: _____

Student name: _____   Grade: _____

Accident or illness description:

_____

_____

_____

_____

_____

_____

_____

Teacher or paraprofessional response:

_____

_____

_____

_____

_____

_____

_____

_____

Parent/guardian notified: Yes   or   No

Teacher's signature: _____

Form A.4   Medical Incident Log

School year: _____

Date	Student Name	Description of Injury or Illness	Teacher's Response

Resource B

Stress Management for the First-Year Teacher

The first-year teacher will quickly discover that the profession of special education can be both physically and emotionally demanding. Stress is a fact of life for most teachers; the enormous caseloads, continuous documenting of student progress, meeting the emotional and academic needs of students, and the threat of litigation, however, are some of the contributing factors to the job-related stress experienced by teachers in the special education profession. Seaward (as quoted in Massey, 1998) defined stress as "the inability to cope with a perceived or real (or imaginary) threat to one's mental, physical, emotional, and spiritual well-being [sic] which results in a series of physiological responses" (p. 1). The simple definition of stress is the body's reaction to the demands placed on it. A certain amount of stress is helpful to keep individuals focused on the job or problem; stress that impedes the teacher's ability to function in the school setting and effectively serve students is counterproductive, however. The authors believe that if the teacher experiences prolonged, elevated levels of job-related stress, the result could lead to job burnout.

The beginning teacher must be able to effectively manage workplace stress to survive the entire school year. The special education teacher must identify his or her stress source and then implement effective stress management strategies. The following are sources of stress identified by Zunker (1994) that the authors found to be most applicable to the special education teaching profession:

- Conditions of work (unpleasant work environment, necessity to work fast, and excessive and inconvenient hours)
- Work itself (perception of job as uninteresting, repetitive, overloaded, and demanding)
- Supervision (unclear job demands, close supervision with no autonomy, and scant feedback from supervisors)
- Role ambiguity (lack of clarity about one's job and scope of responsibilities)

- Group stressor (insufficient group cohesiveness and poor group identity in the organization)
- Organizational structure (too bureaucratic or too autocratic)

The authors provide the reader with suggestions for stress management (Resource B.1) at the end of the chapter.

Finally, the authors suggest that teachers who continue to have difficulty with stress management enroll in staff development courses designed to teach stress management strategies to school employees. The authors strongly urge the beginning teacher to contact his or her school administrator or special education director if all attempts at stress reduction have failed.

Resource B.1   Tips for Stress Management

- Schedule moments of reflection and stress management daily. Rise early, and allow more time for personal reflection before the workday begins.

- Recognize stressful situations quickly, analyze personal feelings, breathe deeply, and loosen muscles.

- When stress builds, use deep breathing techniques and progressive muscle relaxation exercises to reduce tension.

- Learn the strategies of conflict management.

- Learn and be willing to say "No."

- Ask for help.

- Focus on an immediate goal, and work on it until it is completed.

- Try a new activity.

- Talk to significant other.

- Pay attention to health, diet, and sleep needs.

- Exercise daily.

(Continued)

Resource B.1 (Continued)

- Exercise.

- Leave your teaching at school.

- Do not schedule all your leisure time.

- Pursue a project or hobby.

- Find a friend.

- Do not procrastinate.

- Do not feel that you must do everything.

- Keep a "things to do" list.

- Recognize and accept your limitations.

- Learn to tolerate and forgive.

- Learn to plan.

- Be a positive person.

- Learn to play.

- Rid yourself of worry.

SOURCE: Reprinted with permission from Georgia Association of Educators.

Resource C

Support Organizations for Students

Accent on Information (AOI)
P.O. Box 700
Bloomington, IL 61702
Betty Garee, Editor
Telephone: 309-378-2961
Fax: 307-378-4420
e-mail: cheeverpub@aol.com

Advocates for Communication
Technology for Deaf/
Blind People (ACT)
P.O. Box 652
Columbia, MD 21045
Telephone: 410-381-3377

American Amputee Foundation
(AAF)
Box 250218, Hillcrest Station
Little Rock, AR 72225
Jack M. East, Executive Director
Telephone: 501-666-2523;
501-666-9540
Fax: 501-666-8369

American Association of People
With Disabilities (AAPD)
1819 H Street NWE, Ste. 330
Washington, DC 20006
Telephone: 202-457-8168
Toll free: 800-840-8844
Fax: 202-457-0473
Web site: www.aapd.com

Assistance Dogs of America,
Inc. (ADAI)
8806 State Rte. 64
Swanton, OH 43558
Dino Brownson, President
Telephone: 419-825-3622
Toll free: 800-841-2254
Web site: www.adai.org

Council of Citizens With
Low Vision (CCLV)
1400 N. Drake Road, No. 218
Kalamazoo, MI 49006
Elizabeth Lennon, Liaison
Telephone: 616-381-9566
Toll free: 800-733-2258

Direct Link for the Disabled
c/o Linda Lee Harry
P.O. Box 1464
Solvang, CA 93464-1464
Telephone: 805-688-1603;
805-686-5384
Fax: 805-686-5285
e-mail: suharry@terminus.com

Just One Break (JOB)
120 Wall Street
New York, NY 10005
Mikki Lam, Executive Director
Telephone: 212-785-7300
Fax: 212-785-4513

Learning Disabilities
Special Interest
Group (LDSIG)
Westork Community
College
P.O. Box 3649
Fort Smith, AR 72903
Zanette Douglas,
Contact
Telephone: 501-788-7667

National Center for Youth With
Disabilities (NCYD)
University of Minnesota
Division of General Pediatrics
and Adolescent Health
Box 721
420 Delaware Street SE
Minneapolis, MN 55455
Telephone: 612-626-2825
Fax: 612-626-2134

Resource D

Guide to Locating Instructional Materials

A. D. D. Warehouse
300 NW 70th Avenue, Suite 102
Plantation, FL 33337
Telephone: 800-233-9273
Fax: 954-792-8545
Web site: www.addwarehouse.com

Academic Communication
    Associates, Inc.
Publication Center, Dept. 62E
4149 Avenida de la Plata
P.O. Box 4279
Oceanside, CA 92052-4279
Telephone: 760-758-9593
Fax: 760-758-1604

Academic Therapy Publications
20 Commercial Boulevard
Novato, CA 94949-6191
Telephone: 415-883-3314
Fax: 415-883-3720
Web site: www.academictherapy.com

Addison Wesley Longman
    Publishing Co.
1 Jacob Way
Reading, MA 01867
Telephone: 800-552-2499
Fax: 800-284-8292
Web site: www.aw-bc.com

American Guidance Service (AGS)
4201 Woodland Road
Circle Pines,
    MN 55014-1796
Telephone: 800-328-2560
Fax: 612-786-9077
Web site: www.agsnet.com

Attainment Company
P.O. Box 930160
Verona, WI 53593-0160
Telephone: 800-327-4269
Fax: 800-942-3865

Bureau for At-Risk Youth
135 Dupont Street
P.O. Box 760
Plainview,
    NY 11803-0760
Telephone: 800-999-6884
Fax: 516-349-5521
Web site: www.at-risk.com

C. H. Stoelting Co.
620 Wheat Lane
Wood Dale, IL 60191
Telephone: 630-860-9700
Fax: 630-860-9775
Web site: www.stoeltingco
    .com/tests

Cambridge Development
  Laboratory, Inc.
86 West Street
Waltham, MA 02451
Telephone: 800-637-0047
Fax: 781-890-2894

Capstone Curriculum Publishing
151 Good Counsel Drive
P.O. Box 669
Mankato, MN 56002-0669
Telephone: 888-574-6711
Fax: 888-574-6183

Center on Education and Work
  University of Wisconsin–Madison
School of Education
964 Educational
  Sciences Building
1025 W. Johnson Street
Madison, WI 53706-1796
Telephone: 800-446-0399
Fax: 608-262-9197

Channing L. Bete Co., Inc.
200 State Road
South Deerfield, MA 01373-0200
Telephone: 877-896-8532
Fax: 800-499-6464
Web site: www.channing-bete.com

Child's Work Child's PLAY
Genesis Direct Inc.
100 Plaza Drive
Secaucus, NJ 07094-3613
Telephone: 800-962-1141
Fax: 201-583-3644

Curriculum Associates
5 Esquire Road, N
Billerica, MA 01862-2589
Telephone: 800-225-0248
Fax: 800-366-1158
Web site: www.curriculum
  associates.com

EBSCO Curriculum Materials
Box 11521
Birmingham, AL 35202-1521
Telephone: 800-633-8623
Fax: 205-991-1482

Educational Design
345 Hudson Street
New York, NY 10014-4502
Telephone: 800-221-9372
Fax: 212-675-6922

Educators Publishing Service, Inc.
31 Smith Place
Cambridge, MA 02138
Telephone: 800-225-5750
Fax: 617-547-0412
Web site: www.epsbooks.com

Funtastic Therapy
RD 4 Box 14, John White Road
Cranberry, NJ 08512
Telephone: 800-531-3176
Fax: 609-275-0488

Glencoe/McGraw-Hill
P.O. Box 508
Columbus, OH 43216
Telephone: 800-334-7344
Fax: 614-860-1877
Web site: www.glencoe.com

Globe Fearon Publishers
4350 Equity Drive
P.O. Box 2649
Columbus, OH 43216
Telephone: 800-848-9500
Fax: 614-771-7361

Greenwood Publishing
  Group, Inc.
88 Post Road West
Westport, CT 06881
Telephone: 203-226-3571
Fax: 203-222-1502
Web site: www.greenwood.com

Hawthorne
    Educational Services
800 Gray Oak Drive
Columbia, MO 65201
Telephone: 800-542-1673
Fax: 800-442-9509

Huby's Ltd.
School to Work Catalog
Department W99
P.O. Box 9117
Jackson, WY 83002
Telephone: 800-543-0998
Fax: 800-518-2514

J. Weston Walch Publishers
321 Valley Street
P.O. Box 658
Portland, ME 04104-0658
Telephone: 800-341-6094
Fax: 207-772-3105

Kaplan Concepts for
    Exceptional Children
P.O. Box 609
1310 Lewisville-Clemmons Road
Lewisville, NC 27023-0609
Telephone: 800-334-2014
Fax: 800-452-7526
Web site: www.kaplanco.com

Lakeshore Learning Materials
2695 East Dominquez Street
P.O. Box 6261
Carson, CA 90749
Telephone: 800-421-5354
Fax: 310-537-5403
Web site: ww.lakeshorelearning.com

PCI Educational Publishing
2800 NE Loop
    410, Suite 105
San Antonio, TX 78218-1525
Telephone: 800-594-4263
Fax: 888-259-8284
Web site: www.pcicatalog.com

Prufrock Press
P.O. Box 8813
Waco, TX 76714-8813
Telephone: 800-998-2208
Fax: 800-240-0333
Web site: www.prufrock.com

Remedia Publications
10135 East Via Linda, Suite D124
Scottsdale, AZ 85258-5312
Telephone: 800-826-4740
Fax: 602-661-9901
Web site: www.rempub.com

Research Press
P.O. Box 9177
Champaign, IL 61826
Telephone: 800-510-2707
Fax: 217-252-1221
Web site: www.researchpress.com

Resources for Educators
P.O. Box 362916
Des Moines, IA 50336-2916
Telephone: 800-491-0551
Fax: 800-835-5327

Saddleback Educational, Inc.
3503 Cadillac Avenue, Building F-9
Costa Mesa, CA 92618-2767
Telephone: 949-860-2500
Fax: 949-860-2508

Scholastic, Inc.
P.O. Box 7502
Jefferson City, MO 65102
Telephone: 800-724-6527
Fax: 573-635-7630

Scott Foresman/Addison Wesley
School Services
1 Jacob Way
Reading, MA 01867
Telephone: 800-552-2259
Fax: 800-333-3328
Web site: www.sf.aw.com

Slosson
P.O. Box 280
East Aurora, NY 14052-0280
Telephone: 888-756-7766
Fax: 800-655-3840
Web site: www.slosson.com

SRA/McGraw-Hill
220 East Danieldale Road
DeSoto, TX 75115-2490
Telephone: 800-843-8855
Fax: 214-228-1982
Web site: www.sra-4kids.com

Teacher Ideas Press
P.O. Box 6633
Englewood, CO 80155-6633
Telephone: 800-237-6124
Fax: 303-220-8843
Web site: www.lu.com

Things for Learning
P.O. Box 908
Rutherfordton, NC 28139
Telephone: 800-228-6178
Fax: 704-287-9506

Western Psychological Services
12031 Wilshire Boulevard
Los Angeles, CA 90025
Telephone: 800-648-8857
Fax: 310-478-7838

Wieser Educational Inc.
30085 Comercio
Rancho Santa Margarita, CA
        92688-2106
Telephone: 800-880-4433
Fax: 800-949-0209

Resource E

Pharmacology Reference List

The pharmacology information contained here is intended to serve only as a reference source and not as treatment recommendations by the authors. The new teacher should consult a medical professional or school psychologist with questions or concerns pertaining to a particular drug therapy.

Table E.1   Depression

Brand Name[a]	Generic Name[a]	Usual Daily Dose (mg)[b]
Elavil, Endep	Amitryptyline	75–150
Asendin	Amoxapine	200–300
Norpramin, Pertofrane	Desipramine	75–200
Adapin, Sinequan	Doxepin	75–150
Prozac	Fluoxetine	20–80
Janimine, SK-Pramine, Tofranil	Imipramine	50–200
Marplan	Isocarboxazid	10–30
Ludiomil	Maprotiline	75–150
Aventyl, Pamelor	Nortriptyline	75–100
Nardil	Phenelzine	15–30
Vivactil	Protriptyline	15–40
Parnate	Tranylcypromine	20–30
Desyrel	Trazodone	150–600

Table E.2   Anxiety

Brand Name[a]	Generic Name[a]	Usual Daily Dose (mg)[b]
Xanax	Alprazolam	0.75–1.5
BuSpar	Buspirone	15–30
Librium	Chlordiazepoxide	15–40
Tranxene	Clorazepate	30
Valium	Diazepam	4–40
Paxipam	Halazepam	60–160
Ativan	Lorazepam	2–6
Miltown, Equanil	Meprobamate	1200–1600
Serax	Oxazepam	30–60
Centrax	Prazepam	20–40

Table E.3   Attention Deficit Disorder, Attention Deficit Hyperactivity Disorder

Brand Name[a]	Generic Name[a]	Usual Daily Dose (mg)[c]
Ritalin	Methylphenidate	5–60
Cylert	Pemoline	56.25–75
Dexedrine	Dextroamphetamine	2.5–40

Table E.4   Epilepsy

Brand Name[a]	Generic Name[a]	Usual Daily Dose (mg)[c]
Diamox	Acetazolamide	8–30
Tegretol	Carbamazepine	400–800
Klonopin	Clonazepam	0.01–0.2
Valium	Diazepam	1–2.5
Dilantin	Diphenylhydantoin	5–300
Mysoline	Primidone	125–250

SOURCE: a. Poling, Gadow, and Cleary (1991, pp. 149-152).

b. Lickey and Gordon (1991, pp. 380-382).

c. Sifton, Larbi, Kelly, and Perin (1996, pp. 145-581).

References

INTRODUCTION

Daugherty, R. F. (2003). Reflections from first-year teachers: References from Sallie Mae award winners [Electronic version]. *Education, 123*(3), 458–462.

Gordon, S. P. (1991). *How to help beginning teachers succeed.* Alexandria, VA: Association for Supervision & Curriculum Development.

Whitaker, S. D. (2001). Supporting beginning special education teachers. *Focus on Exceptional Children, 34*(4), 1–18.

CHAPTER 1

Daugherty, R. F. (2003). Reflections from first-year teachers: References from Sallie Mae award winners [Electronic version]. *Education, 123*(3), 458–462.

Fore, C., Martin, C., & Bender, W. (2002). Teacher burnout in special education: The causes and the recommended solutions. *High School Journal, 86*(1), 36–45. Retrieved February 22, 2004, from http://web22.epnet.com/citation.asp?tb= 1&_ug=dbs+aph+sid+E3C66E67%2DC7C5%2D4A

French, N. K. (2002). Maximize paraprofessional services for students with learning disabilities. *Intervention in School and Clinic, 38*(1), 50–55.

Friend, M., & Bursuck, W. (2002). *Including students with special needs: A practical guide for classroom teachers.* Boston, MA: Allyn & Bacon.

Sabella, R. A., & Booker, B. L. (2003). Using technology to promote your guidance and counseling program among stake holders [Electronic version]. *Professional School Counseling, 6,* 206–214.

Salend, S. J. (2001). *Creating inclusive classrooms: Effective and reflective practices.* Upper Saddle River, NJ: Prentice Hall.

CHAPTER 2

Boehner, J. (2003). *"No child left behind" emphasizes results, expands options for children with special needs* [Fact sheet]. Retrieved March 3, 2004, from House Education & the Workforce Committee Web site: http://edworkforce.house.gov/issues/ 108th/education/nclb/specialneeds.htm

Bureau of Jewish Education of San Francisco, the Peninsula, Marin and Sonoma Counties. (n.d.). *Special education handbook—Models.* Retrieved April 12, 2004, from http://bjesf.org/MAIN/SpecialEducation/models.html

Gearheart, B. R., Mullen, R. C., & Gearheart, C. J. (1993). *Exceptional individuals: An introduction.* Belmont, CA: Wadsworth.

Grossman, H. J. (Ed.). (1983). *Classification in mental retardation*. Washington, DC: American Association on Mental Deficiency.

Haraway, D. (2002). In their own words: The lessons we learn if we hear. *Preventing School Failure, 46*(2), 57–61.

Kaplan, H. I., & Sadock, B. J. (1991). *Synopsis of psychiatry: Behavioral sciences, clinical psychiatry* (6th ed.). Baltimore, MD: Williams & Wilkins.

Mastropieri, M. A. (2001). Is the glass half full or half empty? Challenges encountered by first-year special education teachers [Electronic version]. *Journal of Special Education, 35*(2), 66–75.

Olson, L. (2004). Special education is the theme of '04 quality counts. *Education Week*. Retrieved May 10, 2004, from http://www.edweek.org/ew/ewstory.cfm?slug= 16QC.h23&keywords=Olson

Schildroth, A. N., & Karchmer, M. A. (1986). *Deaf children in America*. Austin, TX: Pro-Ed.

Smith, D. D., & Luckasson, R. (1992). *Introduction to special education teaching in the age of challenge*. Needham Heights, MA: Allyn & Bacon.

U.S. Department of Education. (1999). *Assistance to states for the education of children with disabilities and the early intervention program for infants and toddlers with disabilities; Final regulations*. Fed. Reg. 64, No. 48, pp. 12421–12422.

CHAPTER 3

Arlington County Public Schools. (1999). Testing and evaluation tips. In *LD OnLine: Testing and Evaluation Tips*. Available: http://www.ldonline_indepth/teaching_ techniques/testin_tips.html

Bureau of Jewish Education of San Francisco, the Peninsula, Marin and Sonoma Counties. (n.d.). *Special education handbook—Models*. Retrieved April 14, 2004, from http://www.bjesf.org/MAIN/SpecialEducation/models.html

Polloway, E. A., Epstein, M. H., & Bursuck, W. D. (2003). Testing adaptations in the general education classroom: Challenges and directions. *Reading and Writing Quarterly, 19*, 189–192.

Rizzo, J. V., & Zabel, R. H. (1988). *Educating children and adolescents with behavioral disorders: An integrative approach*. Needham Heights, MA: Allyn & Bacon.

Roberts, J. (1999). Classroom management for ADD/ADHD students (and other behavioral problems). In *Teachers helping teachers*. Available: http://www.pacificnet.net/ ~mandel/SpecialEducation.html

Smith, D. D., & Luckasson, R. (1992). *Introduction to special education teaching in the age of challenge*. Needham Heights, MA: Allyn & Bacon.

CHAPTER 4

Berdine, W. H., & Cegelka, P. T. (1980). *Teaching the trainable retarded*. Columbus, OH. Charles E. Merrill.

Brackes, C. E., & Ellis, I. C. (2003, May). The secret of classroom management. *Techniques*, 22–25.

Canter, L., & Canter, M. (1995). Assertive discipline. In C. H. Wolfgang (Ed.), *Solving discipline problems: Methods and models for today's teachers* (p. 255). Needham Heights, MA: Simon & Schuster.

Koorland, M. (1995). The behavior analysis model. In C. H. Wolfgang (Ed.), *Solving discipline problems: Methods and models for today's teachers* (p. 149). Needham Heights, MA: Simon & Schuster.

Lewis, R. B., & Doorlag, D. H. (2003). *Teaching special students in general education classrooms*. Upper Saddle River, NJ: Pearson.

Marzano, R. J., & Marzano, J. S. (2003). The key to classroom management. *Educational Leadership, 61*(1), 6–13.

Mercer, C. D., & Mercer, A. R. (1993). *Teaching students with learning problems.* New York: Macmillan.

Miller, S., Wackman, S., Nunnally, E., & Miller, P. (1988). *Connecting with self and others.* Littleton, CO: Interpersonal Communication Programs.

Salend, S. J. (2001). *Creating inclusive classrooms: Effective reflective practices.* Upper Saddle River, NJ: Merrill Prentice Hall.

Wong, H. (1991). *The effective teacher.* Sunnyvale, CA: Wong.

CHAPTER 5

Mercer, C. D., & Mercer, A. R. (1993). *Teaching students with learning problems.* New York: Macmillan.

Southern Regional Education Board. (2001). *Instructional strategies: How teachers teach matters* (No. 01V23). Atlanta, GA: Author.

Thompson, M., & Thompson, J. (2003). *Learning-focused strategies notebook* [Workbook]. Boone, NC: Learning Concepts.

U.S. Department of Education. (1996, Spring). What are promising ways to assess student learning? In *Improving America's Schools: A Newsletter on Issues in School Reform.* Retrieved April 5, 2004, from http://www.ed.gov/pubs/IASA/newsletters/assess/pt.3.html

CHAPTER 6

Berger, E. (1995). *Parents as partners in education: Families and schools working together.* Englewood Cliffs, NJ: Prentice Hall.

Miller, S., Wackman, S., Nunnally, E., & Miller, P. (1988). *Connecting with self and others.* Littleton, CO: Interpersonal Communication Programs.

Minke, K., & Anderson, K. (2003). Restructuring routine parent-teacher conferences: The families-school conference model. *Elementary School Journal, 104*(1), 49–69.

Morehead, M. A. (2001). *Dealing with the anger of parents.* Retrieved January 8, 2004, from New Mexico State University Web site: http://education.nmsu.edu/departments/academic/ci/morehead/handouts/angry.html

Shea, I. M., & Bauer, A. M. (1991). *Parents and teachers of children with exceptionalities.* Needham Heights, MA: Allyn & Bacon.

CHAPTER 7

Browder, D., Flowers, C., Ahlgrim-Delzell, L., Karvonen, M., Spooner, F., & Algozzine, R. (2004). The alignment of alternate assessment content with academic and functional curricula. *Journal of Special Education, 37*(4), 211–223.

Buros Institute of Mental Measurement test reviews online. (n.d.). Retrieved April 23, 2004, from http://buros.unl.edu/buros/jsp/reviews.jsp?item=06000003

Canter, A. (1998). Understanding test scores: A handout for teachers. *National Association of School Psychologists,* pp. 119–120.

Carr, J. F., & Harris, D. E. (2001). *Succeeding with standards: Linking curriculum, assessment, and action planning.* Alexandria, VA: Association for Supervision and Curriculum Development.

Florida Department of Education, Division of Public Schools and Community Education, Bureau of Instructional Support and Community Services. (1998, July). *Guidelines for determining modifications for use on state and district assessments for students with disabilities* [Technical assistance paper]. Tallahassee, FL: Author.

Individuals with Disabilities Education Act of 1975, Pub. L. No. 105-117. Fed. Reg. 64, No. 48, 1999.

Linn, J. E., & Gronlund, M. A. (1995). *Measurement and assessment in teaching.* Englewood Cliffs, NJ: Prentice Hall.

Mehrens, W. A., & Lehmann, I. J. (1987). *Using standardized tests in education.* White Plains, NY: Longman.

Sweetland, R. C., & O'Connor, W. (Eds.). (1984). *Tests: A comprehensive reference for assessments in psychology, education and business.* Kansas City, MO: SKS Associates.

Thurlow, M. L., Elliott, J. L., & Ysseldyke, J. E. (1998). *Testing students with disabilities: Practical strategies for complying with district and state requirements.* Thousand Oaks, CA: Corwin.

CHAPTER 8

House Education & the Workforce Committee. (2003, April 9). *"No child left behind" emphasizes results, expands options for children with special needs.* Retrieved March 3, 2004, from http://edworkforce.house.gov/issues/108th/education/nclb/special needs.htm

House Education & the Workforce Committee. (2003, April 28). *The Improving Education Results for Children with Disabilities Act: Separating fact from fiction.* Retrieved March 3, 2004, from http://edworkforce.house.gov/issues/108th/education/idea/factvsfiction.htm

Individuals with Disabilities Education Act of 1975, Pub. L. No. 105-117. Fed. Reg. 64, No. 48, 1999.

Mager, R. F. (1984). *Preparing instructional objectives.* Belmont, CA: Pitman.

Mason, C. Y., McGahee-Kovac, M., & Johnson, L. (2004). How to help students lead their IEP meetings. *Teaching Exceptional Children, 36*(3), 18–25.

CHAPTER 9

Bliss, P. (2003, November 3). School to work units. *Paula's Special Education Resources.* Retrieved April 30, 2004, from http://www.paulablis.com/stwgoals.htm

Job Accommodation Network. (2004, January). *Job accommodations for people with mental retardation (MR) or other developmental disabilities,* JAN'S Accommodation Fact Sheet Series. Retrieved April 30, 2004, from http://janweb.icdi.wvu.edu

Kohler, P., & Field, S. (2003). Transition-focused education: Foundation for the future. *Journal of Special Education, 37*(3), 174–183.

Mager, R. F. (1984). *Measuring instructional results or got a match?* (2nd ed.). Belmont, CA: Lake.

A primer on IDEA and its regulations. (1999). *CEC Today, 5*(7), 5.

Queen, J. A. (2002). *Student transitions from middle to high school: Improving achievement and creating a safer environment.* Larchmont, NY: Eye on Education.

U.S. Department of Education, Office for Civil Rights. (2002). *Students with disabilities preparing for postsecondary education: Know your rights and responsibilities.* Washington, DC: Author.

Wehman, P. (1996). *Life beyond the classroom* (2nd ed.). Baltimore, MD: Brookes.

CHAPTER 10

Covey, S. R. (1992). *Principle-centered leadership.* New York: Simon & Schuster.

RESOURCE A

National Safety Council. (1992). *First aid and CPR* (2nd ed.). Boston: Jones & Bartlett.

RESOURCE B

Georgia Association of Educators. (1998). *Avoiding burnout and staying healthy.* Available: http://smhp.psych.ucla.edu/qf/burnout_qt/avoidburn.pdf

Massey, M. S. (1998). *Promoting stress management: The role of the comprehensive school health programs.* Washington, DC: ERIC Clearinghouse on Teaching and Teacher Education. (ERIC Document Reproduction Service No. ED421480)

Zunker, V. G. (1994). *Career counseling: Applied concepts of life planning* (4th ed.). Pacific Grove, CA: Cole.

RESOURCE E

Lickey, M. E., & Gordon, B. (1991). *Medicine and mental illness: The use of drugs in psychiatry.* New York: Freeman.

Poling, A., Gadow, K., & Cleary, J. (1991). *Drug therapy for behavior disorders: An introduction.* Elmsford, NY: Pearson Allyn & Bacon.

Sifton, D., Larbi, A., Kelly, G., & Perin, T. (Eds.). (1996). *The PDR family guide to prescription drugs* (4th ed.). Montvale, NJ: Medical Economics.

Index

**CORWIN
PRESS**

The Corwin Press logo—a raven striding across an open book—represents the union of courage and learning. Corwin Press is committed to improving education for all learners by publishing books and other professional development resources for those serving the field of K–12 education. By providing practical, hands-on materials, Corwin Press continues to carry out the promise of its motto: **"Helping Educators Do Their Work Better."**